Theoreticians and Builders

Theoreticians and Builders

Mathematicians, Physical Scientists, Inventors

Judy McClure

RAINTREE
STECK-VAUGHN
PUBLISHERS

A Harcourt Company

Austin   New York
www.steck-vaughn.com

Published by Raintree Steck-Vaughn Publishers, an imprint of
Steck-Vaughn Company

CREATED IN ASSOCIATION WITH MEDIA PROJECTS INCORPORATED
C. Carter Smith, *Executive Editor*
Carter Smith III, *Managing Editor*
Judy McClure, *Principal Writer*
Ana Deboo, *Project Editor*
Bernard Schleifer, *Art Director*
John Kern, *Cover Design*
Karen Covington, *Production Editor*

RAINTREE STECK-VAUGHN PUBLISHERS STAFF
Walter Kossmann, *Publishing Director*
Kathy DeVico, *Editor*
Max Brinkmann, *Art Director*

Photos on front cover, clockwise from top left: Sally Ride, Etta Zuber Falconer,
Lene Vestergaard Hau, Marie Curie

Photos on title page, top to bottom: Maria Agnesi, Ellen Swallow Richards,
Adriana Ocampo, Chien-Shiung Wu

Acknowledgments listed on page 80 constitute part of this copyright page.

Library of Congress Cataloging-in-Publication Data
McClure, Judy.
    Theoreticians and builders: mathematicians, physical scientists,
    inventors / Judy McClure.
        p.   cm.—(Remarkable women: past and present)
    Includes index.
    ISBN 0-8172-5728-4
    1. Women physical scientists—Biography—Juvenile literature. 2. Women
mathematicians—Biography—Juvenile literature. 3. Women inventors—Biography—
Juvenile literature. [1. Mathematicians. 2. Physical scientists. 3. Inventors. 4. Scientists.
5. Women—Biography.] I. Title. II. Series: Remarkable women.
Q141.M3575   2000
500.2'092'2—dc21   00-027839
[B]   CIP

Printed and bound in the United States
1 2 3 4 5 6 7 8 9 0 LB 03 02 01 00

CONTENTS

INTRODUCTION

Even today in America, educators puzzle over a phenomenon called "math phobia." Although girls and boys perform equally well in math and sciences at first, by high school more girls than boys have lost interest in those topics. People have suggested that the female brain works differently, making it more difficult for girls to do math or use visualization to solve technical problems. But "math phobia" doesn't exist in all world cultures. Besides, there is ample evidence—as you will see when you read this book—that women make excellent mathematicians, physicists, chemists, astronomers, engineers, and architects. It may surprise you to discover how ardently many of them love science. When physicist Lene Vestergaard Hau was in college, she preferred doing math to going to the movies.

It wasn't very long ago that science was considered an unfeminine pursuit. The movie star Hedy Lamarr hid the fact that she had helped create an important invention, perhaps because she thought it would tarnish her glamorous image. Donna Shirley's college adviser told her not to major in engineering. If she hadn't ignored him, she would never have supervised the creation of *Sojourner*, the rover that arrived on Mars in 1998 and broadcast pictures of the planet back to Earth.

When faced with career obstacles, many past women scientists chose to collaborate with men. Sophia Brahe assisted her famous brother, astronomer Tycho Brahe. Mathematician Mary Everest Boole worked with her husband, George. At the Harvard Observatory in the 19th century, a group of exceptionally talented women astronomers that included Annie Jump Cannon, Antonia Maury, and Henrietta Leavitt performed the background research that helped confirm the more spectacular theories of their male colleagues. And before the invention of that ubiquitous electronic device, the computer, teams of mathematicians, usually women, spent their careers as "calculators."

Many scientifically inclined women chose invention as their outlet. Even if they didn't have a formal scientific education, they would conceive of a useful object and learn what they needed to know to make it happen. Scholars point out that women inventors must have been active for millennia. After all, who is more likely to invent a loom: the man who hunts all day, or the woman who weaves cloth? Even so, the names of many female inventors are lost because their ideas weren't documented. Elena Popescu devised a tool to help an elderly woman thread a needle, not to make a fortune selling the gadget. Often husbands reaped the benefits of their wives' work. Hannah Slater, the wife of a famous industrialist, invented the cotton thread that helped make him wealthy, but few details of her life survive.

Some women inventors focused on making "women's work" easier. Lillian Moller Gilbreth created such devices as the electric mixer; Patsy Sherman invented a stain-repelling fabric treatment that must have saved countless hours of scrubbing. Other women inventors' works aren't particularly "feminine." Kate Gleason devised ways of using concrete for building projects. Katherine Burr Blodgett invented glare-proof glass, which has many applications in optical equipment.

Outstanding work receives the recognition it deserves. Pioneers like chemist Dorothy Crowfoot Hodgkin, physicist Lise Meitner, and computer scientist Grace Murray Hopper inspired deep respect among their colleagues. Marie Curie and her daughter, Irène Joliot-Curie, who studied radiation, were considered as brilliant as any male scientist. Curie was the first two-time Nobel Prize–winner of either sex, and Joliot-Curie captured a third Nobel for the family. Thanks to the precedent they and other technologically minded women have set, girls who love science have many exciting career options—and they should never let "math phobia" get in their way.

Photos top left Donna Shirley, bottom left Emily Roebling,
top right Lillian Moller Gilbreth, bottom right Evelyn Granville

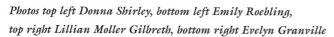

Aglaonike (5th century B.C.E.?)
Astronomer, priestess

Aglaonike lived in the region of Thessaly in ancient Greece. Little is known about her except that she claimed to be able to make the moon disappear. This feat was a tradition among women in her community. They were considered sorceresses.

Of course Aglaonike and the other women weren't causing the moon to disappear; they were accurately predicting lunar eclipses. A lunar eclipse occurs when the moon, Earth, and sun fall in a straight line. The Earth blocks the light from the sun, casting a shadow on the moon, which then *seems* to disappear. Aglaonike may have used the eclipse cycle recorded by the ancient Babylonians on clay tablets in the ninth century B.C.E. It is also possible that the Thessalonian women, who had long worshiped the goddess of the moon, created their own records and passed them down for generations.

People were awed by Aglaonike's story for centuries. Finally the Greek historian Plutarch, who lived during the late first and early second centuries, pointed out that she must have had knowledge of the cycles of the moon rather than magical powers.

Maria Gaetana Agnesi (1718–1799)
Mathematician, philosopher

Maria Agnesi was an important figure of the scientific revolution in Italy. From a young age she entertained friends of her father, a professor of mathematics at the University of Bologna, by speaking about scientific subjects. The girl was able to respond to many visitors in their own languages, because she was fluent in Latin, Greek, French, Spanish, Hebrew, and German.

Maria's brilliance in mathematics and languages was matched by her religious fervor. When she was 20, she wanted to enter a convent. Her father persuaded her not to by agreeing to allow her to lead a simple and religious life. She spent the next years studying and writing about math.

Agnesi's most famous work, the textbook *Instituzioni analitiche ad uso della gioventù Italiana* (1748, Analytical institutions for the use of Italian youth), was used for over 100 years. It included explanations of many new theories of algebra and

calculus. Empress Maria Theresa of Austria, to whom Maria dedicated the book, sent her a diamond ring and a letter in a crystal case. Pope Benedict XIV recognized her work with a gold medal.

After Agnesi's father died in 1752, she abandoned mathematics and dedicated her life to religion and charity. She founded a home for the elderly in Milan, became its director, and lived there for the remainder of her life.

Betsy Ancker-Johnson (1929–)
Physicist

After spending four happy years at Wellesley College in Massachusetts, Betsy Ancker decided to attend graduate school in Germany. Her experience at Tübingen University turned out to be difficult. She was often told there that women had no aptitude for physics. She persevered, though, and in 1953 graduated with a Ph.D.

Back home in America, her job hunt was equally frustrating. She was finally hired as a lecturer at the University of California at Berkeley, where she met her future husband, mathematician Hal Johnson. Soon she moved on to research positions at Radio Corporation of America and Boeing Aerospace Company. She established herself as an expert in the study of plasma (charged particles that resemble gas

Scientist and Mother

Betsy Ancker-Johnson insisted on having a career and a family, but she encountered obstacles along the way. The first time she became pregnant, she was working at a research laboratory in New Jersey. One day she visited the infirmary to have a small burn bandaged. A nurse, appalled to see the expectant scientist, persuaded the company to fire her (she was later rehired). When Ancker-Johnson had her second child, her job at Boeing was secure. But the company, following state law, stopped her paycheck for a mandated 14-week maternity leave although she worked for most of that time.

but conduct electricity) in solids and obtained several patents while at Boeing. She and her husband had two children and adopted two more. They worked hard to balance their careers and family.

In 1973 Ancker-Johnson became assistant secretary of science and technology at the United States Department of Commerce. General Motors hired her six years later as vice-president of environmental activities, and she remained there until her retirement in 1992.

Elda Emma Anderson (1899–1961)
Physicist

IN 1941 DR. ELDA EMMA ANDERSON, A PHYSICIST on leave from her teaching job in Wisconsin, was working at Princeton University's Office of Scientific Research and Development. That year, the United States entered World War II. Soon Anderson was summoned to the Los Alamos Lab in New Mexico to work on the top-secret "Manhattan Project" to create an atomic bomb.

Powerful explosions can be created through fission, or splitting the nucleus of an atom, when an element such as uranium or plutonium is used. The explosion is deadly, and the resulting radiation can cause harm for a long time afterward. Anderson and her colleagues successfully created the first atomic bomb. It was tested in the desert in August 1945. The United States dropped two atomic bombs on Japan the following month.

Radiation proved to have beneficial uses in medicine, industry, and energy. Because of the dangers associated with it, a new field emerged, health physics. Anderson became the first chief of education at Oak Ridge National Laboratory's Health Physics Division in Tennessee. Her research focused on ways to protect people who worked with radiation. It included determining safe degrees of exposure and methods for disposing of radioactive waste.

Exposure to radiation may have caused Anderson's death. In 1956 she discovered she had leukemia, and later she was diagnosed with breast cancer. Still, she continued her career for as long as possible. She is remembered by an annual award given in her name by the Health Physics Society to an outstanding health physicist.

Mary Anning (1799–1847)
Paleontologist

THE TONGUE TWISTER "SHE SELLS SEASHELLS ON the seashore" is said to be about Mary Anning. She did live by the sea, in Lyme Regis, England, but she was selling fossils—not shells. Her father, a carpenter, loved collecting fossils and inspired Mary. After his death in 1810, she continued on her own.

When Mary was 12, she and her brother found some bones sticking out of a cliff. Mary worked hard to dig out the bones without breaking them. It turned out that she had discovered the complete remains of an ichthyosaur, an extinct marine reptile. In 1824 she became the first to discover an almost complete skeleton of another ancient reptile, the plesiosaur. Her work became well known among paleontologists, and she began selling the fossils that she found.

Anning's working-class background and the fact that she was female probably kept her from receiving the recognition she deserved. She finally gained financial support in 1838, when the British Association for the Advancement of Science agreed to pay her an annual stipend. After her death from breast cancer, the Geological Society printed her obituary in their quarterly journal, even though they would not admit women for another seven years.

Hertha Marks Ayrton (1854–1923)
Physicist, inventor

SARAH MARKS WAS BORN TO A JEWISH FAMILY IN Portsmouth, England, but changed her first name to Hertha while attending Girton College. Although she was never very good at taking examinations, she went on to become a renowned inventor and a physicist.

Hertha's career began with inventing. In 1884 she patented a "line divider." This drafting tool was used to divide a line into equal parts and was useful for architects, artists, and engineers. She also entered Finsbury Technical College, where she met a professor of physics named W. E. Ayrton. They were married the following year.

Hertha Ayrton's work became well known. Her paper "The Mechanism of the Electric Arc" was read to the Royal Society (England's foremost scientific organization) in 1901—as a woman, she wasn't allowed to present it herself. Her book, *The Electric Arc* (1902), became the standard text on the topic.

Ayrton went on to study and write about the movement of waves and the formation of ripples in the sand. This time, in 1904, the Royal Society invited her to present her own paper on the subject. Although Ayrton was never accepted as a member, in 1906 she became the first woman scientist to receive the Royal Society's prestigious Hughes Medal for original research.

Active until the end of her life, Ayrton was an enthusiastic member of the suffrage movement. When World War I broke out, she created her famous "Ayrton Fan" to remove poisonous gases from the soldiers' trenches.

June Bacon-Bercey (1934–)
Meteorologist

MORE THAN ONCE JUNE BACON-BERCEY WAS advised to reconsider her plans to become a meteorologist—few, if any, African American women had ever entered that field. Still, she graduated with a master's degree from the University of California at Los Angeles in 1955 and was hired by the National Weather Service in Washington, D.C. While there she developed forecasting charts that were used around the world. She went on to work with the Sperry Rand Corporation and to become a television correspondent at NBC.

In 1977 Bacon-Bercey appeared on the television game show *The $128,000 Question* and won the grand prize. She used the money to establish a scholarship, administered by the American Geophysical Union, for young women who hope to become atmospheric scientists. After serving as chief administrator of television activities for the National Oceanic and Atmospheric Administration, Bacon-Bercey became a forecasting training officer at the National Weather Service in California.

Bacon-Bercey began devoting herself full-time to encouraging young scientists in 1990. She has worked with schools, foundations, and government organizations to create educational programs on meteorology. She and her husband, physician George Brewer, have two children.

Nina Karlovna Bari (1901–1961)
Mathematician

WHEN MOSCOW STATE UNIVERSITY REOPENED in 1918 after the Russian Revolution, Nina Bari was the first woman to take advantage of the school's new coeducational policy. She joined several other students who had mathematics professor Nikolai Nikolaevich Luzin as a mentor. The

"Luzitanians," as they called themselves, became leaders in the new abstract approach to mathematics.

Bari was probably the first woman graduate of the university. She finished early—in 1921—and began teaching. After Moscow State established its Research Institute of Mathematics and Mechanics, she returned for graduate work, while continuing to teach and forging a brilliant career. In 1922 she became the first woman to present a lecture to the Moscow Mathematical Society. Her thesis on the theory of trigonometric series received the 1926 Glavnauk Prize. She studied in Europe from 1927 to 1929, spending much of that time in Paris.

Bari returned to Moscow State University and became a popular professor. She published many articles and textbooks, including her final work, a 900-page book on trigonometry. Bari was married to mathematician Viktor Nemytski. They spent much of their free time together hiking in the mountains of the Soviet Union.

Nora Stanton Blatch Barney (1883–1971)
Civil engineer, architect, suffragist

Nora Blatch was the daughter of Harriot Stanton Blatch and the granddaughter of Elizabeth Cady Stanton, both major figures in the women's rights movement. Nora was born in England, but the family eventually settled in New York City, and she entered Cornell University in 1901. She graduated with honors, becoming the first woman in the country to receive a degree in civil engineering. She was also the first woman elected to the American Society of Civil Engineers. Nora was given junior status, which was customary for members of her age. However, when she reached the age for regular membership, she was dropped from the organization. In 1916 she brought a lawsuit demanding her reinstatement but was unsuccessful.

Nora's 1906 marriage to Lee De Forest, inventor of the radio vacuum tube, ended in divorce. She went on to work as an engineer for the Radley Steel Construction Company and the New York Public Service Commission. After marrying her second husband, marine architect Morgan Barney, her interests turned to architecture. By 1923 she was designing and selling expensive houses in Greenwich, Connecticut.

Like her mother and grandmother, Barney was politically involved. She was active in the women's suffrage movement and became president of the Women's Political Union in 1915. Because of her membership in the Congress of American Women, she was suspected of having Communist sympathies and was investigated by the House Committee on Un-American Activities in 1950.

Florence Bascom (1862–1945)
Geologist

Florence Bascom came from a supportive, well-educated family. Both her parents were strongly in favor of women's rights. Her father was president of the University of Wisconsin, where Florence enrolled in 1877. After earning a master's degree in geology, she moved to Baltimore, Maryland, to attend Johns Hopkins University in 1889. Women were not normally accepted there, and she was required to sit behind a screen during classes, so that she wouldn't "distract" the male students. In 1893 she became the first woman to earn a Ph.D. from that university.

Dr. Bascom was the first woman to work with the United States Geological Survey. Her responsibilities involved mapping selected areas of the country. She became an expert in petrology, the classification and description of rocks.

Bascom was a talented teacher. Even before she earned her Ph.D., she taught at the Hampton Institute for Negroes and American Indians and at Rockford College. When she began her long career at Bryn Mawr College in Pennsylvania in 1895, there was no geology department. She created an exceptional department, where many future geologists, including Ida Ogilvie and Julia Gardner, came to study. Many honors were accorded to Florence Bascom during her career, one of which was the inclusion of four stars by her biographical entry in the 1906 edition of *American Men and Women of Science*.

In 1738 she married fellow scientist Giovanni Verati. They had at least eight children. Bassi's research interests included hydraulics and electricity. In addition to her fame as a scientist and teacher, she was known for writing poetry and helping the poor.

One of Bassi's greatest honors was her appointment in 1745 to the Benedettini Academics, an association created for Italy's top scientists. After a successful career, she died unexpectedly a few hours after giving a lecture. The women of Bologna erected a monument honoring her at Bologna's Institute of Sciences.

Laura Bassi (1711–1778)

Physicist, philosopher, natural scientist

Laura Bassi began her formal education at the age of five with her cousin as her teacher. Fifteen years later she was well known for her success in public academic debates. In 1732, having been appointed to the Academy of Sciences in Bologna, her hometown, Bassi debated professors from the university there. Her arguments on 49 different topics in philosophy and science earned her a doctorate and a position as professor.

Bassi spent most of her career at the University of Bologna but also taught at other institutions in Italy.

Jocelyn Bell Burnell (1943–)

Radio astronomer, physicist

As an 11-year-old, Irish-born Jocelyn Bell failed the exam that would have allowed her to pursue an academic education. Although the standard alternative was vocational training, her parents sent her to Mount School, a Quaker girls' school in York, England. Jocelyn developed a love of physics and astronomy and went on to attend the University of Glasgow, graduating with a bachelor's degree in physics.

As a Ph.D. student at Cambridge University, Jocelyn built a radio telescope under the direction of Antony Hewish, her adviser. Hewish was studying

Pulsars

The word *pulsar* is short for "pulsating radio star," a star that emits regular pulses of radio waves. It is believed that pulsars are very dense, rapidly rotating stars made up primarily of neutrons and no larger than 12 miles (20 km) in diameter. These "neutron stars" are created when the core of an exploding star (or supernova) collapses. In the process, protons and electrons are released into the spinning magnetic field surrounding the star. The particles emit electromagnetic radiation, which can be detected by radio telescopes like those used by Jocelyn Bell Burnell and Antony Hewish in 1967.

stars by tracking the radio waves they emitted. In 1967 they turned the telescope on, and it began scanning the sky, producing a 100-foot (30-m) long paper printout daily. Analyzing the marks indicating radio waves, Bell noticed small but regular blips. Most stars emit a constant signal, but something was giving off a pulsing signal.

After checking the equipment to be sure it wasn't malfunctioning—and considering whether extra-terrestrial beings might be responsible—Hewish and Bell decided that the signals were being emitted by rotating neutron stars, or "pulsars." It was a major discovery. In 1973 the Franklin Institute of Philadelphia honored Hewish and Bell with the Albert A. Michelson Medal. However, the 1974 Nobel Prize in physics was given to Antony Hewish alone. Bell married Martin Burnell in 1968. She is currently a professor at the Open University in England.

Ruth Rogan Benerito (1916–)
Physical chemist

ANYONE WHO WEARS COTTON CLOTHING HAS probably benefited from Ruth Benerito's work. She holds more than 50 patents, many of them devoted to processes for making cotton fabrics wrinkleproof, waterproof, stainproof, fire-resistant, or simply more comfortable.

Ruth's father was a civil engineer; her mother was an artist. She graduated early from her high school in New Orleans—at age 14—and majored in chemistry at Sophie Newcomb College, the women's school at Tulane University. After graduating in 1935, she spent a year as a graduate student at Bryn Mawr in Pennsylvania.

Returning to New Orleans, Benerito volunteered at a hospital laboratory, served as a social worker for President Franklin Roosevelt's Works Progress Administration, and taught school. In the evenings she studied with physicist Rose Mooney. In 1943 she began teaching college courses. She held posts at Newcomb and Tulane in New Orleans while working part-time toward her Ph.D. at the University of Chicago. She received the degree in 1948.

In 1953 Benerito began working at Southern Regional Research Center, a laboratory in New Orleans run by the United States Department of Agriculture. She worked on many projects there,

including devising ways to analyze fats and proteins and finding ways to improve cotton fabrics. Her honors include being the first woman to receive the Southern Chemist Award, in 1968.

Evelyn Berezin (1925–)
Computer scientist

EVELYN BEREZIN WORKED HARD TO ESCAPE THE poverty she experienced as a child in the Bronx, New York. She entered college at age 16, intending to study bookkeeping, but a part-time job involving physics soon changed her focus. She eventually received an Atomic Energy Commission fellowship to finance a Ph.D. in physics at New York University. When the fellowship ended, Berezin turned to a new field, electronic data processing.

In 1951 Berezin was hired by the Electronic Computer Corporation, a tiny firm in Brooklyn, and was told to "design a computer." She had never seen one before—few people had at the time—but she came up with the Elecom 200. Two years later, at the Underwood Corporation, she created the first office computer. While working for the Teleregister Corporation during the late 1950s, she devised the first on-line computer reservation service for a commercial airline. Later she developed other high-speed digital communications advances with Digitronics Corporation. In all, she received six patents in her field.

In 1969 Berezin cofounded her own company, Redactron, and produced the "Data Secretary" editing typewriter—an early form of word processor. By 1976 she had changed focus again, entering the field of investment management. She continues to work as a venture capital consultant, helping entrepreneurs with technological business ideas find funding.

Patricia Billings (1926–)
Inventor

IN 1996 IN KANSAS CITY, MISSOURI, FIRE MARSHALS set out to burn down two small buildings. One was made of standard materials; the shingles and roof of the other were made of GeoBond, invented by Patricia Billings. The standard building burst into flames, while the GeoBond one remained cool enough to touch.

Billings had trained as a medical technician at junior college. As a young wife and then a divorcée, she had devoted herself to art while raising her daughter. In the 1970s, after one of her favorite sculptures broke, she decided to create an unbreakable plaster. She thought of the well-preserved 16th-century frescoes (paintings made by applying pigments to moist plaster) she had seen during a vacation in Italy. Through research she discovered that Renaissance artists had used some sort of additive to bind a cementlike material with gypsum (plaster of paris).

It took eight years for Billings to find a substance that worked. The result was, coincidentally, quite fire-resistant. A scientist friend at the U.S. Gypsum Corporation encouraged her to develop the substance further. Eventually she founded her own company, GeoBond International. The product is a promising replacement for asbestos, now banned as a fire retardant in construction because it causes cancer.

Hazel Bishop (1906–1998)
Chemist, inventor

BORN IN HOBOKEN, NEW JERSEY, HAZEL BISHOP inherited an entrepreneurial streak from her father but majored in chemistry at Barnard College in New York City. She began her career as a research

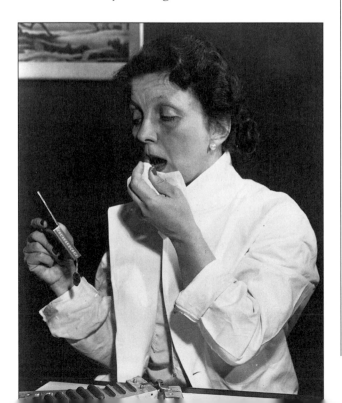

assistant to a dermatologist at Columbia University Medical Center. During World War II, she worked for Standard Oil, developing a special fuel for bomber planes. She then went to Socony Vacuum Oil, where she focused on petroleum research.

In 1950 Bishop introduced her "no-smear" lipstick, which she had created during her spare time in her kitchen. The first day it was available at Lord & Taylor department store, the entire supply was sold. She established Hazel Bishop, Inc., and served as its president until disagreements with her business partner caused her to leave. The dispute deprived her of the right to do business under her own name, as she discovered when she founded Hazel Bishop Laboratories soon afterward.

Later Bishop turned to a financial career, becoming a stockbroker for Bache & Company in 1962. She remained in demand as an adviser to cosmetics manufacturers, though. In 1978 she became a professor at the Fashion Institute of Technology in New York. She continued to mix up small batches of lipstick—in her favorite shade of red—for her personal use.

Mary Adela Blagg (1858–1944)
Astronomer

UNTIL THE EARLY YEARS OF THE 20TH CENTURY, lunar astronomers around the world had a difficult time communicating with one another about their findings. There were no standardized maps of the moon. Astronomer Mary Blagg played an important role in solving that problem.

Blagg was born in North Staffordshire, England, and attended boarding school in London. Upon returning home, she used her brother's textbooks to teach herself mathematics. When she became interested in astronomy, the scientist J. A. Hardcastle helped her become a member of an international committee to standardize information about the moon. Blagg's assignment was to review all the different names for each lunar formation, and she reported her findings in a manual, *Collated List* (1913). Appointed to the Lunar Commission of the International Astronomical Union in 1920, she helped prepare *Named Lunar Formations* (1935), which became the standard for astronomers.

Blagg was also involved with the study of variable stars, whose brightness fluctuates over time. She analyzed data from several astronomers and published her results in ten papers between 1912 and 1918. Like most women scientists of her time, she was not paid, but her work was highly valued. In 1915 she was elected to the Royal Astronomical Society. After her death, a lunar crater was named Blagg in her honor.

Helen Augusta Blanchard (1840–1922)
Inventor

As A CHILD LIVING IN PORTLAND, MAINE, HELEN Blanchard enjoyed creating things, but she never received a formal technical education. Her father operated a prosperous shipping business for many years, but at the time of his death he was nearly bankrupt. Afterward Helen moved to Boston with her sister. There she invented a sewing machine and received the first of her 28 patents in 1873.

Most of Blanchard's inventions were mechanical and were intended for use in factories. Her zigzag stitch sewing machine was the first ever patented. The companies more commonly credited with that invention—Pfaff and Necchi for their home models and Singer for the industrial version—applied for patents after Blanchard's had already expired.

Around 1881 Helen and her sister founded the Blanchard Overseaming Company in Philadelphia. Among her later inventions were a surgical needle and several machines for sewing hats. Her company was quite successful, and she was eventually able to buy back her family's land and her father's business in Maine. Blanchard's 1873 sewing machine is now at the Smithsonian Institution's National Museum of American History in Washington, D.C.

Katherine Burr Blodgett (1898–1979)
Physicist, inventor

IF YOU HAVE EVER LOOKED THROUGH A MICROSCOPE, used a camera, or viewed a valuable painting at a museum, you have benefited from Katherine Blodgett's work. She invented nonreflecting glass.

Blodgett was the first woman scientist hired by the General Electric Research Laboratory, in Schenectady, New York, the town of her birth. At the time, she was only 19 years old. She had already graduated from Bryn Mawr College and earned a master's degree in physics from the University of Chicago. Her supervisor at GE, chemist Irving Langmuir, encouraged her to continue her studies. In 1926 she became the first woman to receive a Ph.D. in physics from England's Cambridge University.

Returning to GE, Dr. Blodgett began the research that would earn her United States patent #2,220,660 in 1938. Langmuir had developed an oily liquid that formed a one-molecule-thick film on water. It was a fascinating property, but none of the scientists had been able to figure out a practical application for the substance. Blodgett found a way to make the thin film adhere to glass. She also discovered that she could stack one layer of the film on top of another—and that once she had applied the right number of layers, the glass no longer reflected light the way normal glass does.

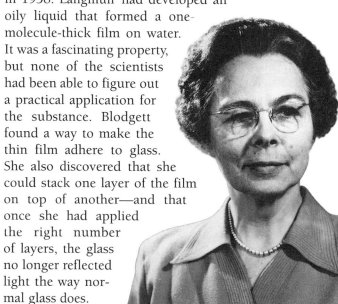

Blodgett remained at GE until she reached the mandatory retirement age of 65. Her discoveries and techniques continue to be used by many scientists and inventors.

Mary Everest Boole (1832–1916)
Mathematical educator

IN 1837 MARY EVEREST'S FAMILY LEFT ENGLAND to live in France, so that her critically ill father could receive homeopathic medical treatments. The experience inspired Mary's lifelong interest in alternative philosophies. She was also influenced by her French tutor, Monsieur Deplace, who taught her mathematics by helping her think out the principles for herself. The family returned to England in 1843, and Mary left school to help her father at the church where he was a minister.

In 1850 Mary visited her uncle in Cork, Ireland, and became friends with mathematician George Boole. They continued to correspond after she returned home, married in 1855, and eventually had five daughters. Mary, who had helped George with his book *Laws of Thought* (1854) during their courtship, continued to collaborate with him.

Mary became increasingly interested in psychology and the ways that people learned mathematics. After George's death in 1864, she worked for several years as a librarian at Queens College in London. Her home became a gathering place for intellectuals. She invented valuable learning tools, such as her patented "curve-sewing cards," used by students to make geometric shapes. During her later years, she wrote a great deal, including *Lectures on the Logic of Arithmetic* (1903) and *The Preparation of the Child for Science* (1904).

> "It may occur to some that too much use is made of examples relating to food. But we cannot make mathematicians by insisting upon a non-existing superiority to physical facts. Apple or bun forms the natural unit for a child, the sharing of a cake or fruit is the natural fraction as well as the true introduction to the higher ethical life. As a matter of fact the Arithmetic of grown people is largely occupied over questions of food supply and of personal or family interest."
>
> MARY EVEREST BOOLE
> Preface to *Lectures on the Logic of Arithmetic*

Sophia Brahe (1556–1643)
Astronomer, horticulturist

SOPHIA BRAHE WAS THE YOUNGEST SISTER OF THE famed astronomer Tycho Brahe. She was well educated and often assisted her brother at his observatory in Uraniborg, Denmark. When she was only 17, Sophia helped Tycho perform the calculations necessary to predict a lunar eclipse. She was also with him to observe and record the event, which took place on December 8, 1573.

Around 1576 Sophia married Otto Thott, and they had one child. Thott died in 1588, and Sophia then managed his property in Eriksholm, while frequently visiting her brother. In 1590 she became engaged to Erik Lange, whom she had met at Tycho's observatory. Lange, an alchemist, had accumulated substantial debts carrying out expensive experiments. He left Denmark for several years to escape his creditors, delaying the marriage until 1602. Sophia went on to become a talented horticulturist and to study alchemy and medicine. She often treated the poor and was well respected in the community. She lived to be 87 years old.

Yvonne Brill (1924–)
Aerospace engineer

AFTER EARNING HER B.S. IN MATHEMATICS FROM the University of Manitoba, Canadian Yvonne Brill was unable to find a job in her home country. Moving to California, she was soon hired by the Douglas Aircraft Company. In the years following World War II, she worked at RAND, a newly established nonprofit research and development organization, studying rocket design and propellant formulas. She completed her master's degree at the

University of Southern California in 1951, the year of her marriage to a fellow scientist.

The young couple settled in Connecticut, and Brill worked part-time while raising their three children. In 1966 she accepted full-time work at RCA Astro-Electronics. There she made several contributions to her field, most notably a design for satellite propulsion that is still in use. RCA honored her with their Astro-Electronics Engineering Excellence Award in 1970.

Brill took two years away from RCA to work for NASA. In 1986 she accepted a position as a space segment engineer at the International Maritime Satellite Organization (INMARSAT) in London. Even after retiring in 1991, Brill continued to serve as a consultant. In 1993 she was honored with the Society of Women Engineers' Resnik Challenger Medal. She was inducted into the Women in Technology International Hall of Fame in 1999.

Harriet Brooks (1876–1933)
Physicist

Harriet Brooks, a native of Exeter, Ontario, earned a teaching diploma from McGill University in Montreal in 1898 and continued on as a graduate student in physics. While studying radioactive materials with her adviser, physicist Ernest Rutherford, she discovered that the element thorium emitted radon gas as it decayed. This was one of the earliest indications that one element could "transmute," or change, into another, something previously considered impossible. In 1901 Brooks became the first woman to earn a master's degree from McGill.

Brooks spent the next year at Cambridge University's Cavendish Laboratory in England, where she determined thorium's half-life, a measurement of an element's rate of decay. She went on to hold various teaching posts, while continuing her research. In 1904 she was hired by Barnard College in New York City.

Brooks might have become as famous as Marie Curie. However, in 1906 she got engaged—and married women weren't allowed to teach at Barnard. Brooks argued with the dean, and although the wedding was called off, she left her job. After working for a year at the Curie Institute in Paris, she married Frank Pitcher, and they had three children. She did not continue her scientific career, but her early research helped to establish the field of atomic physics.

Margaret Burbidge with her daughter Sarah

Margaret Burbidge (1925–)
Astronomer

Margaret Peachey's parents encouraged her interest in science even when she was just a small child. She went on to study astronomy as an undergraduate and graduate student at the University of London. During World War II, while the men served in the army, Margaret cared for the equipment at the university's observatory. In the evenings, after observatory hours, she conducted research for her Ph.D., which she earned in 1943. Five years later she married Geoffrey Burbidge, a fellow astronomer and frequent collaborator in her research.

One of Margaret's interests was studying the elemental metals created during the evolution of stars. In 1959 she, Geoffrey, and two other astronomers won the American Astronomical Society's Warner Prize for work on this topic. Later in her career she focused on calculating the weight of galaxies by using their rotational speed.

Burbidge has spent many years in the United States, especially at the University of California at San Diego, where she began teaching in 1962. In 1972 she took a leave to become the first woman director of the Royal Greenwich Observatory in England, and four years later she became the first woman president of the American Astronomical Society. During the 1980s she began working with NASA, where she helped to develop the Hubble Space Telescope.

Stellar Types

The star classification system devised by Annie Jump Cannon and her colleagues at the Harvard College Observatory has since been modified to accommodate new discoveries, but the basic categories are still used. The astronomers divided stars into seven classes: O, B, A, F, G, K, and M. (Astronomy students often remember the sequence using the phrase "Oh, Be A Fine Guy, Kiss Me.") Their system led to the discovery that stars of the same spectral type have similar surface temperatures. O stars, which are blue, are the hottest; F stars, in the middle range, are white; and M stars, the coolest, are red.

Annie Jump Cannon (1863–1941)
Astronomer

GROWING UP IN DELAWARE, ANNIE CANNON spent many evenings in the attic with her mother, studying the constellations. She was also fascinated by the way light was affected by the prism-like crystals of her parents' elegant candelabra. She attended Wellesley College in Massachusetts and then lived at home for nearly a decade. Devastated by her mother's death in 1893, she turned again to astronomy.

In the late 1800s, Edward Pickering of the Harvard College Observatory assembled a group of women astronomers to help him identify and classify stars. Cannon joined them in 1896 and would remain at Harvard until 1940. Over time she became very deaf, but with hearing aids and lipreading she had no trouble understanding others.

Classifying stars involves photographing them through a prism and analyzing the spectra of light they emit. Cannon helped simplify the classification system to include seven types based on the surface temperature of the star. In all, she classified over 350,000 stars. Her major publications were the nine-volume *Henry Draper Catalogue* (1918–1924) and the two-volume *Henry Draper Extension* (1925, 1949).

Cannon supported women's suffrage and the advancement of women in science. Among her many honors was the 1932 Ellen Richards Prize of the Society to Aid Scientific Research by Women (the last one awarded); she used the money to establish a new award for women through the American Astronomical Society. The Annie Jump Cannon Prize was awarded regularly until the 1970s.

Emma Perry Carr (1880–1972)
Chemist, educator

AFTER EARNING HER BACHELOR OF SCIENCE degree and a Ph.D. from the University of Chicago, Emma Carr accepted a position at Mount Holyoke College in Massachusetts in 1910. She became head of the chemistry department three years later. For over 30 years, she created an atmosphere where cooperation, research, and learning could take place, and she trained many great women chemists.

Dr. Carr led research on organic compounds, especially unsaturated hydrocarbons (carbon compounds that have double or triple bonds). In Europe a technique called ultraviolet absorption spectroscopy was being used to analyze the structure of compounds. Carr traveled to Ireland and Switzerland to learn about it and brought the technique to Mount Holyoke. She, her students, and colleagues used spectroscopy to study carbon-carbon double bonds. Their discoveries led to new theories in organic chemistry and earned important research grants for the department.

Emma Carr's influence extended beyond the chemistry department to the entire college. A spirited

and outspoken person, she served on many committees. She and her colleague Mary Lura Sherrill shared a home and a busy social life. In 1937 Carr became the first recipient of the Garvan Medal of the American Chemical Society. She retired at age 65 but remained active at the college and in her community.

Jessie Whitney Cartwright (1897–1977)
Inventor

JESSIE CARTWRIGHT SPENT MOST OF HER CAREER AS director of the National Home Services Division at Norge, where her inventions helped improve technology in the home. Although she is only named on one patent—for the "Ripplette" washing machine agitator for delicate clothes—she was involved with several other inventions. Her contributions included the Radarange microwave oven, a refrigerator icemaker, and a stop cycle for dryers. One of her most important improvements was to put a metal panel on the back of washers and dryers. This device protected the machinery and shielded the consumer from electrical shocks.

Cartwright had studied home economics while at Michigan State University. She raised three daughters before beginning her career. After her retirement from Norge in 1966, she was immediately hired to supervise the women's division of the United States pavilion at the International Trade Fair in Italy.

Beyond her contributions to technology, Cartwright was renowned as a suffragist, teacher, and humanitarian. In a time of racial segregation, she convinced the William Penn Hotel in Pittsburgh to give a suite to the African American actress and singer Lena Horne. Cartwright was elected to Chicago's Hall of Fame in 1972.

Émilie, Marquise du Châtelet (1706–1749)
Mathematician, writer, philosopher

BORN INTO THE FRENCH ARISTOCRACY, GABRIELLE-Émilie Le Tonnelier de Breteuil married Marquis Florent-Claude du Châtelet at age 19. The marriage provided her with the wealth and freedom to lead a flamboyant and intellectually stimulating life. Although the couple had three children, they lived mostly apart. Émilie's great love was the philosopher and writer Voltaire.

In 1738 Émilie set up a home laboratory to study the nature of fire for an essay competition sponsored by the Academy of Sciences. As part of her investigation, she disproved the commonly held theory that heat was a material substance by showing that objects did not get heavier as they burned. She didn't win the competition, but the Academy published her essay.

Émilie's textbook, *Institutions de physique* (1740, The foundations of physics), began as a study aid for her son. In it she combined the theories of the scientists Sir Isaac Newton and Gottfried Leibniz and provided definitions and historical background. Among the few people she confided in while she was writing it was her former tutor, Samuel König—who then announced to the public that he had dictated the book to Émilie. She disputed his claim and was eventually confirmed as the author.

At age 43 Émilie became pregnant for the fourth time. Sensing that she would not survive the childbirth, she worked feverishly, completing her translation of Newton's *Principia Mathematica* (1687, Mathematical principles) days before her death. The two-volume work was published in 1759 and, for a long time, was the only French translation available.

Edith Clarke (1883–1959)
Electrical engineer

AN ORPHAN BY THE TIME SHE WAS 12 YEARS OLD, Edith Clarke was raised by her sister Mary on their Maryland farm. She used her portion of the family inheritance to attend Vassar College and graduated in 1908. After studying civil engineering at the University of Wisconsin, she took a job at American Telephone & Telegraph (AT&T) in New York City. Computers did not yet exist, so the complicated calculations that are central to engineering had to be performed by people. At AT&T, Clarke supervised these human "computers."

In 1919 Clarke became the first woman to earn a master's degree in electrical engineering from the Massachusetts Institute of Technology. Then she began a long career at General Electric. The focus of her work was to use mathematics to simplify engineering problems. She developed a calculating device, patented in 1925, to help engineers predict how power systems would perform during difficult conditions. She also published often, most notably the graduate-level textbook *Circuit Analysis of A-C Power Systems* (1943).

Clarke retired from GE in 1945, but she soon accepted a position as a professor of electrical engineering at the University of Texas in Austin. In 1948 she became the first woman member of the American Institute of Electrical Engineers.

Josephine Cochrane (1842?–after 1908)
Inventor

ALTHOUGH JOSEPHINE COCHRANE WAS NOT THE first to patent a dishwasher, hers was the first commercially available model. A housewife who lived in Shelbyville, Illinois, she worked on designs for several years and received patents in 1886, 1888, and 1894. She established one of America's first companies for kitchen equipment. Having undergone several mergers and changes in owners, the business survives today in the brand Kitchenaid.

Cochrane exhibited her dishwashers at the 1893 World's Columbian Exposition in Chicago. By then she had created two models, one for the home and one for restaurants. The latter, powered by a steam engine, could clean and dry over 200 dishes in two minutes. Cochrane also exhibited her machines in New York City in 1908 at an event called the Martha Washington Hotel Suffrage Bazaar.

Like many women inventors, Cochrane did not manage to establish lasting fame. Few details of her life other than her name and patent listings have survived. She is the best known of the 30 or so women who patented dishwashers or improvements to the machines in the late 19th century.

Martha J. Coston (1826–1906)
Inventor

MARTHA COSTON MARRIED AS A TEENAGER. When she was 21, her husband, mother, and youngest child died, leaving her alone in Washington, D.C., with three children to support. The grieving widow turned to her husband's journal for comfort. There she found a promising business idea— a sketch of a signal flare to be used by ships at night.

It took years for Coston to make the idea into a working reality. She decided that three colors of flares were needed in order to devise an effective communication code. Under a man's name, she wrote to fireworks experts for advice. In 1859 she received patent #23,536 in her husband's name for "Pyrotechnic Night Signals." The green, red, and white flares are credited with helping the North win the Civil War.

Orders poured in, and rather than manufacture the flares herself, Coston sold the patent to the United States Congress for $20,000. In 1871 she received a patent in her own name for a flare holder, and later her son Harry developed a flare gun. Coston always felt that a man would have been paid more for the same work. Still, she prospered as a result of her inventions and was able to raise her children in style.

Marie Curie (1867–1934)
Physicist, chemist

MARIE CURIE WAS BORN MARYA SKLODOWSKA IN Russian-controlled Warsaw. Her mother died of tuberculosis in 1877, and Marie formed a strong bond with her father, a physics teacher. In 1891 she enrolled at the Sorbonne in Paris. Within three years she earned two master's degrees. She also met Pierre Curie, a fellow physicist. They married in 1895 and

would eventually have two daughters.

Marie was fascinated by the discovery of the radioactive element uranium by physicist Henri Becquerel and used his findings as a starting point for her doctoral research. Together with Pierre, she began the difficult task of isolating radioactive elements, working in a makeshift lab. Using a method Marie invented, they extracted the elements polonium and radium from mineral ores. In 1903 both Curies and Becquerel received the Nobel Prize in physics.

In 1906 Pierre was killed in a traffic accident. Although devastated, Marie took over the classes he had been teaching at the Sorbonne. By this time she had begun to experience illness caused by exposure to radiation—now known to be very dangerous. She ignored her discomfort and continued her research. In 1911 she became the first person to win a second Nobel Prize, this time for chemistry.

During World War I, Marie and her daughter Irène developed medical uses for X rays. She spent her later years traveling with her daughters and giving lectures. In 1934 she died of leukemia, probably caused by overexposure to radiation. She did not live to see Irène win the Nobel Prize in 1935.

Christine Darden (1942–)
Aerospace engineer

ONE DAY CHRISTINE DARDEN'S FATHER WATCHED her fix a bicycle and was so pleased with her skill that her gave her a set of tools. While at high school in North Carolina, she took as many math classes as possible. She would have liked to take shop—but only boys were allowed. As an African American woman, she was discouraged from being a scientist, so she majored in education.

Darden taught high school, then worked at Virginia State College while she earned her master's degree in mathematics. After graduating in 1966, she was hired by NASA as a data analyst. Later she was promoted to an aerospace engineer, and she earned her doctorate in engineering from George Washington University in 1983.

In 1989 Dr. Darden became the leader of the Sonic Boom Group at NASA. A sonic boom occurs when an airplane surpasses the speed of sound. The thunderous noise produced can be loud enough to damage buildings. Only military aircraft are allowed to fly at supersonic speeds over land in the United States. Darden and her group are working to design aircraft that produce less disruptive sonic booms, so that many people can take advantage of the speed of supersonic travel.

Olive Dennis (1885–1957)
Engineer

AT THE CORNELL UNIVERSITY GRADUATION ceremony where Olive Dennis received her master's degree in engineering, she heard a bystander say, "Now what the heck can a woman do in engineering?" The year was 1920. Dennis, who had grown up in Baltimore building toys and reading her brother's engineering books, went on to do great things.

The Baltimore and Ohio Railroad hired Dennis as a draftsperson for their bridge department. She soon became a service engineer, a post dedicated to improving the environment for passengers. At the time, train travel was uncomfortable and dirty. If the windows were open, smoke and cinders from the burning coal that powered the train flew inside. If they were closed, the passengers had no fresh air.

Dennis solved the problem by inserting individual ventilation systems into the wall below each window. Her other inventions included headrests and footrests, reclining seats, lunch counters, and even a patented china design for the Baltimore and Ohio's 100th anniversary. Because she tested all innovations herself, Dennis spent many hours traveling on the railroad she helped to revolutionize.

Marion Donovan (1917–1998)
Inventor

MARION DONOVAN'S FATHER INVENTED A TOOL for producing automobile gears, and as a girl she spent many afternoons at his factory in Fort Wayne, Indiana. However, she didn't follow his inventive example right away. She was a magazine editor at *Vogue* until she married and left work to raise her children. One day, fed up with leaky cloth diapers, she decided to make a waterproof diaper cover.

She sewed her first prototype out of a shower curtain. Three years later, the Boater, as she called it, had plastic snaps and was made of nylon. Manufacturers showed little interest, so Donovan financed the project herself. In 1951 she sold the patent rights for $1 million. Her next idea, to create a disposable diaper out of absorbent paper, was ridiculed by paper company executives. It would be ten years before another innovator, Victor Mills, began manufacturing such diapers.

Donovan returned to school and earned an architecture degree from Yale University in 1958. She also continued inventing. Among her many useful devices were the Big Hangup, which held 30 items and saved closet space, and the Dentaloop, which made flossing teeth a more comfortable task.

Mildred Spiewak Dresselhaus (1930–)
Physicist

MILDRED SPIEWAK WAS BORN TO A POOR immigrant family living in New York City. She loved learning, especially science and music. Determined to get a top-notch education, she prepared herself for the Hunter College High School entrance exam and earned a perfect score in math. Later she attended Hunter College, where her adviser, Dr. Rosalyn Yalow, encouraged her to become a scientist. She graduated in 1951 and spent a year studying physics at the Cavendish Laboratory in Cambridge, England.

In 1958, the year she married physicist Gene Dresselhaus, Mildred received her Ph.D. from the University of Chicago. Two years later the young couple were offered jobs at the Massachusetts Institute of Technology's Lincoln Laboratory. Mildred's research there included studying the electronic properties

of graphite, a common form of carbon. In 1968 she became a professor at MIT, a position that gave her greater opportunities for research and more flexibility for raising her four children.

Dresselhaus worked hard to bring more women students to MIT. She also developed a Women's Forum to discuss issues faced by all women and to promote their careers. In 1985 she was made an Institute Professor, a lifetime title awarded to only 12 MIT faculty members at a time. She has received many other honors, including the 1990 National Medal of Science.

Jeanne Dumeé (17th century)
Astronomer

THERE WERE SEVERAL IMPORTANT WOMEN astronomers during the 17th century. Most worked with their husbands or brothers, but Jeanne Dumeé worked alone. Dumeé, who lived in Paris, was only 17 years old when her soldier husband was killed in battle. Afterward she decided to study science.

Dumeé's observations of Venus and the moons of Jupiter supported the theories of astronomer Nicolaus Copernicus. In the early 1500s, Copernicus had challenged the popular belief that the Earth was the center of the universe and that the sun rotated around it. About a century later, Galileo Galilei and Johannes Kepler confirmed that, in fact, Earth and the other planets revolve around the sun. Dumeé's work during the 1680s provided even more evidence of that.

Dumeé also hoped to prove to a skeptical public that women were as capable of scientific learning as men and argued this point in her writings. Her manuscript won praise from other scientists but was never published.

Mileva Maric Einstein (1875–1948)
Physicist

PERHAPS IN A DIFFERENT TIME MILEVA MARIC would have become almost as famous as her husband, physicist Albert Einstein. But during the late 1800s, aspiring women physicists received little support. Personal problems and depression, in part due to her unhappy relationship with Einstein, added to Maric's difficulties.

As a high school student in Zagreb, Croatia, Maric's scientific talent earned her special permission to attend a boys' school. She went on to study in Switzerland, where women had greater access to higher education. She met Einstein at the Swiss Federal Polytechnic Institute in Zurich. A blissful romance followed, and they married in 1903. She abandoned her studies, and the couple's happiness gradually faded. By 1910 she was busy keeping house and raising two sons.

Some researchers think Maric contributed to Einstein's work. In several letters he refers to three papers written in 1905 as "our work." One of these papers earned Einstein the Nobel Prize in 1921. Although they were divorced by then, he gave Maric all the award money. Maric's last years were shadowed by her own failing health and her youngest son's mental instability. As a young woman, she had said that she would never marry because that would make it impossible for her to have a career. It seems her prediction about the effect marriage would have on her life was correct.

Mileva Einstein with Albert Einstein

Thelma Estrin (1924–)
Electrical engineer

WHEN AMERICA ENTERED WORLD WAR II, Thelma and Gerald Estrin had just married. He went off to fight. Left to support herself in New York City, she began looking for a job. Although her aptitude test scores indicated that she should avoid engineering, Thelma took a course in it and was hired by the Radio Receptor Company. After the war ended in 1945, the Estrins moved to Madison, Wisconsin. Over the next six years, Thelma earned her bachelor's, master's, and Ph.D. degrees in electrical engineering at the university there.

Dr. Estrin got a job at the Neurological Institute at Columbia Presbyterian Hospital, where she discovered her area of specialty: studying the uses of computers to record and analyze brain activity. While working at the Weizmann Institute in Israel in 1954, she helped build the Middle East's first electronic computer. In the 1960s Estrin, by then the mother of three daughters, accepted a position at the University of California at Los Angeles Brain Research Institute.

Estrin held several posts at UCLA. In 1984 she was appointed assistant dean of the School of Engineering and Applied Sciences. During this time she worked to support and promote women in engineering, technology, and management. She retired from teaching in 1991.

Carrie J. Everson (1844?–1913)
Inventor, mineralogist

LIKE MANY OTHER AMERICANS SEEKING THEIR fortune, Massachusetts-born Carrie Everson and her family went west during the Gold Rush. They settled in Colorado, where Carrie worked as a schoolteacher and helped her husband look for gold.

Hoping to improve their chances of success, Carrie began experimenting with ways to separate ore—mineral that contained substantial quantities of the precious metal—from the surrounding rock. She found that agitating crushed rock in a mixture of oil, water, and certain acids would cause the valuable bits of mineral to float, while the useless rock sank to the bottom. In 1886 she earned a patent for this "oil flotation" separation process. She also collaborated with Charles Hebron, and they were granted two more patents for related inventions.

Everson never profited from her innovations, and ended up working as a nurse in California. While her patents were active, gold and silver deposits were plentiful enough that it wasn't necessary to extract the metals from crushed ore. Her methods were later adapted by engineers to extract silver, gold, copper, and other valuable metals from large amounts of crushed rock. By that time her patents had expired.

Etta Zuber Falconer (1931–)
Mathematician, educator

Etta Zuber left the segregated South in 1954 to attend graduate school at the University of Wisconsin in Madison. She had earned her undergraduate degree in mathematics from Fisk University, where one of her most inspiring teachers was Evelyn Boyd Granville. But Zuber felt lonely in

Wisconsin; African American women academics were so rare that the students in the course she taught laughed at her on the first day. Although the class turned out well and she earned her master's degree, she decided to return home to Mississippi. She accepted a teaching position at Okolona Junior College, where she met her husband, Dolan Falconer.

In 1964 she was hired as an assistant professor at Spelman College in Georgia. At the same time, she attended graduate courses at Emory University and completed her Ph.D. in 1969 with a focus on algebra. In 1972 Dr. Falconer became chair of the mathematics department at Spelman. She instituted several innovative programs, including summer classes to expose young women to opportunities in math and science.

Falconer has worked hard to attract more African American students to mathematics and other sciences. She was recognized for these efforts with the 1995 Louise Hay Award, given by the Association for Women in Mathematics.

Edith Flanigen (1929–)
Chemist

Edith Flanigen graduated in 1950 from D'Youville College in Buffalo, New York, with the top grades in her class. Two years later she earned her master's degree in inorganic chemistry from Syracuse University and was hired by the Linde Division of Union Carbide Corporation. During her long career at Linde, Flanigen made great advances in synthesizing chemical substances.

In 1956 she developed a method for making large quantities of zeolite Y, an important petroleum-refining catalyst. After petroleum is extracted from the earth as crude oil, it must be separated into usable parts, or "fractions." Zeolite Y is used to produce gasoline. The 200 different substances developed or invented by Flanigen not only made gasoline production safer and more efficient; they have been used in environmental cleanups and water purification. She also helped devise a way to synthesize emeralds.

Flanigen has earned 102 patents in all. In 1992 she became the first woman awarded the Perkin Medal by the Society of Chemical Industry's American Section. This honor, decided by officers from several chemistry associations, recognizes outstanding contributions to applied chemistry.

Williamina Paton Stevens Fleming (1857–1911)

Astronomer

Raised in Scotland, Williamina Fleming followed an unusual career path to become one of the first women astronomers at the Harvard College Observatory in Massachusetts. Although she was originally a schoolteacher, after immigrating to America in 1878 and divorcing her husband, she accepted a job as a housekeeper to support her young son. Her employer was Edward Pickering, director of the Harvard observatory. Pickering needed a reliable research assistant and gave Fleming simple tasks. Her talent and interest in astronomy were obvious, and in 1881 he hired her as a full-time researcher.

Fleming's primary task was to create a new classification system for stars by examining photographs taken through a prism to reveal their spectra—a process known as spectroscopy. The classification system she developed would be further refined by Annie Jump Cannon, who also worked at the observatory.

In addition to classifying 10,351 stars in her book, *The Draper Catalogue of Stellar Spectra* (1907), Fleming identified 222 variable stars, or stars whose brightness varies over time. She also discovered 10

novae (stars that suddenly become very bright and then fade again) and 59 nebulae (clouds of gas and dust in space).

Fleming was appointed curator of astronomical photographs at the Harvard College Observatory in 1898 and spent much of her time in later years as an administrator and supervisor. She hired many women astronomers, including Antonia Maury and Henrietta Leavitt. She is remembered as an extraordinary astronomer and an advocate for women scientists.

Irmgard Flügge-Lotz (1903–1974)

Aeronautical engineer, mathematician

Like other German children, Irmgard Lotz enjoyed going to the movies. Unlike the other kids, however, Irmgard preferred to watch technical films about engineering. Her father was a mathematician, and her mother's family operated a successful construction company.

Irmgard put herself through the Technische Hochschule (technical university) in Hanover by tutoring other students, and she received her Ph.D. in engineering in 1929. Her dissertation focused on thermodynamics.

Lotz began her engineering career at the Aerodynamische Versuchsanstalt (aeronautical research institute) in Göttingen. There she developed the "Lotz method" for calculating an airplane wing's lifting force. In 1938 she married Wilhelm Flügge, another engineer. Although both opposed the Nazi regime, they performed aerodynamics research for the German government during World War II. In 1947 they moved to Paris and after a year accepted jobs at Stanford University in the United States.

Dr. Flügge-Lotz is probably best known for her work in automatic flight control. Although other engineers had determined how to increase the speed of airplanes, they still had to be controlled manually. Her theory of discontinuous control systems, or systems that have on and off switches, led to the development of jets. In 1960 Flügge-Lotz was the only woman delegate at an international conference on flight control in Moscow. Ten years later she became the second woman member of the American Institute of Aeronautics and Astronautics.

Beatrice Fu (1958–)
Engineer

BEATRICE FU WAS BORN IN HONG KONG, BUT she moved to the United States so that she could attend college at the California Institute of Technology. After she graduated in 1980, a few people tried to discourage her from studying engi-

neering because she was a woman, but she merely considered their remarks a challenge. Perhaps because her family always supported her interest in science, she never doubted she would succeed.

After earning her master's degree from the University of California at Berkeley, Fu began her career with the Intel Corporation, a manufacturer of computer circuitry. She worked in a variety of positions, including semiconductor-chip manufacturing, microprocessor design, and software development. For several years she was a manager, supervising 200 engineers and their projects. By that time her home life was quite busy as well; she had married a fellow engineer, and they had two sons. In 1997 Fu became vice-president of engineering for Tensilica, Inc. Her new business' goal is to provide a way for companies to customize computer hardware according to their needs.

Elizabeth Fulhame (18th century)
Chemist

BRITISH SCIENTIST ELIZABETH FULHAME STARTED out to create fabric using gold and silver. Her husband, Thomas, and other scientist friends doubted the endeavor would work, but after many experiments, she had some success. She also devised a way to bind metal to paper, like paint. Then she decided to investigate the theoretical aspects of her work.

Influenced by Antoine and Marie Lavoisier's work with combustion, Fulhame theorized that water (made up of hydrogen and oxygen molecules) made certain chemical reactions possible, and that, although water decomposed during the reactions, the same amount of it was regenerated afterward. For example, she suggested that as charcoal burned, the oxygen molecules in water facilitated the combustion, while the hydrogen molecules were released into the air to combine with more oxygen—forming water again. Her experiments supported her theory, and in 1794 she published *An Essay on Combustion*.

The book, with its meticulously documented experiments, gained her much respect as a chemist. In America the Philadelphia Chemical Society declared her an honorary member. Mysteriously, though, her fame did not last, and few details of her life have been preserved. Scientist Jöns Jakob Berzelius coined the term "catalysis" in 1836 to describe the process Fulhame wrote about, and he is often credited with being the originator of the theory.

Frances GABe (1915–)
Inventor

NOT MANY PEOPLE ENJOY HOUSEWORK, CERTAINLY not Frances GABe, who invented the Self-Cleaning House (SCH). As the unusual spelling of her pseudonym, GABe, indicates, the inventor is an individualist. Born in Idaho, she left her parents' home when she was 13 years old—not to run away, but to attend a polytechnic school. She began working on the SCH as a young mother. Now divorced, she has spent decades creating the 68 patented devices that operate the house. Her home in Oregon serves as her laboratory. She also envisions other self-cleaning buildings, including hospitals and public restrooms.

The main feature of the SCH is the General Room-Washing Apparatus, which sprays a warm soap-and-water mist, rinses, and uses hot air to dry the room. Other features include a Dishwasher Cupboard that allows the owner to put dirty dishes directly back into the storage area, where they are washed, dried, and made ready for the next meal.

GABe, who has not yet found a financial backer to produce her invention, does not want the SCH to

> "Men decided a few centuries ago that any job they found repulsive was women's work. They didn't want to clean up someone else's dirt either, and who can blame them? How clever it was of them to find a way to make someone else do it instead. But in all fairness, why me instead of you? Why you instead of me? Housework is a thankless, unending job—a nerve-twanging bore. Who wants it? Nobody."
>
> FRANCES GABE
> "The GABe Self-Cleaning House," 1983

be a luxury item. She has designed it so that the average family could afford to buy one. It would also be beneficial to the elderly and disabled, who often have to leave their homes when they can no longer care for them.

Sulochana Gadgil (1944–)
Meteorologist

SULOCHANA PHATAK WAS BORN IN PUNE, INDIA. She earned her bachelor's degree in chemistry and her master's degree in mathematics from Poona University. In 1965 she married Madhav Gadgil, a fellow student from the university. They traveled together to the United States to attend Harvard University, where Sulochana earned her Ph.D. in mathematics. By the time she wrote her doctoral dissertation, she was already interested in meteorology; she chose to analyze the movement of the Gulf Stream (a warm ocean current in the North Atlantic) using her mathematical training. In 1973 Gadgil joined the faculty at the Indian Institute of Science. She became chair of the institute's Centre for Atmospheric Sciences 16 years later.

The main focus of Gadgil's research has been monsoons, seasonal winds that have especially strong effects in southern Asia and Africa. Monsoons there bring heavy rainfall, and Gadgil has studied their effect on Indian life and agriculture, as well as analyzing the meteorological phenomena associated with them. The author of more than 40 articles, she received the B. N. Desai Award from the India Meteorological Society in 1982. Outside of her work, Dr. Gadgil is interested in bird-watching and Indian classical music.

Diana Garcia-Prichard (1949–)
Chemical physicist

DIANA GARCIA WAS BORN IN SAN FRANCISCO to a Nicaraguan mother and a Mexican American father. She was four years old when she performed her first scientific experiment: Desperate to understand how a toy worked, she took it apart. Even so, she did not find the right outlet for her talents immediately. After graduating from high school, Garcia became a nurse but soon decided the job didn't suit her. She married, had two children, and divorced. In 1979 her brother encouraged her to return to school.

At California State University at Hayward, Diana enjoyed the challenge of her science classes. She also met her second husband, Mark Prichard. She earned a bachelor's degree in chemistry and physics and went on to graduate school at the University of Rochester in New York. There she participated in important research on the behavior of gases that do not follow the known gas laws. She received her Ph.D. in chemical physics in 1988.

Garcia-Prichard now works as a research scientist for Eastman Kodak. She has many commitments outside of research, as well. These include membership in the Society for Hispanic Professional Engineers and work with Latinas Unidas, a group that helps Hispanic and Latin women reach their goals.

Julia Anna Gardner (1882–1960)
Geologist, paleontologist

JULIA GARDNER BELONGED TO THE EARLY GENERATION of women geologists who studied with Florence Bascom at Bryn Mawr College. Her primary research interest was mollusks, and she spent a summer at the Woods Hole Marine Biological Laboratory in Massachusetts. She received her Ph.D. in paleontology from Johns Hopkins University in 1911.

Geologic Time

The oldest rocks date back nearly four billion years, and geologists have created a special calendar to organize the vast expanse of time between then and the present. The units are (in order of decreasing length) eons, eras, periods, and epochs. Julia Gardner studied the Oligocene epoch, which belongs to the Phanerozoic eon, the Cenozoic era, and the Tertiary period. During the epoch there was an increase in grasslands, which allowed for the development of herbivores (grass-eating animals) such as primitive horses, pigs, and camels.

For many years Dr. Gardner worked with the United States Geological Survey (USGS) researching the Atlantic Coastal Plain, a lowland area that stretches along the eastern seacoast from Massachusetts to Mexico. Her first project, in 1914, was to categorize mollusk fossils from the Oligocene epoch (a geologic period that spanned the time from 36.6 to 23.7 million years ago). Many other studies followed. When the Coastal Plain projects ended, Gardner moved to the USGS paleontology and stratigraphy section, where she analyzed the composition of sedimentary rock by examining the fossils in its layers.

During World War I and its aftermath, Gardner interrupted her work and volunteered in France with the Red Cross and the American Friends Service Committee until she was injured in 1919. She also served in World War II, this time as a member of the USGS Military Geology Unit. Part of her work involved determining the origin of balloon-borne Japanese bombs by analyzing the contents of the sandbags used to balance the balloons.

Hilda Geiringer (1893–1973)
Applied mathematician

HILDA GEIRINGER'S PARENTS SUPPORTED HER interest in mathematics by sending her to the University of Vienna, and in 1917 she graduated with a Ph.D. She became an assistant to Richard von Mises at the Institute of Applied Mathematics in Berlin. She also married but divorced soon after the birth of her daughter, Magda.

In 1927 Dr. Geiringer became a lecturer at the University of Berlin. She was nominated for a prestigious promotion in 1933, but that same year Adolf Hitler came to power. Geiringer, like all other Jewish faculty, lost her job. She went to Belgium and then to Turkey, where she taught at the University of Istanbul for five years. In 1939 she obtained a position at Bryn Mawr College in Pennsylvania and moved with Magda to the United States.

In 1943 Geiringer married von Mises, who by then lived in Massachusetts and worked at Harvard University. Geiringer accepted a faculty post at nearby Wheaton College. In the evenings she continued her own research, focusing on statistics and probability. When her husband died in 1953, she received a grant to complete his research at Harvard. In 1967 the University of Vienna honored her with a celebration marking the 50th anniversary of her graduation.

Margaret Joan Geller (1947–)
Astronomer

AS A CHILD MARGARET GELLER LOVED VISITING HER father and his colleagues in physics at Bell Laboratories in Morristown, New Jersey. She spent her undergraduate years at the University of California at Berkeley and then studied astrophysics at Princeton University. In 1975 she became the second woman ever to receive a Ph.D. in physics from Princeton.

Geller has spent most of her career at Harvard University, working with astronomer John Huchra to create a three-dimensional map of a large portion of the universe. To do this, they use redshift surveys, in which the wavelengths of the light emitted by galaxies are analyzed to determine the galaxies' distance from Earth. Most scientists, including Geller, expected to find the galaxies in an orderly arrangement, but by 1985 she and Huchra had realized that the opposite was true. They are clumped together like bubbles, leaving large, empty spaces. One gigantic cluster, which they named the Great Wall, is over 500 million light-years long but only 15 million light-years wide.

In 1990 Dr. Geller received a prestigious "genius" grant from the MacArthur Foundation. In an effort to

help the general public understand astronomy, she joined filmmaker Boyd Estus to create two documentaries, *Where the Galaxies Are* (1991) and *So Many Galaxies . . . So Little Time* (1992).

Sophie Germain (1776–1831)
Mathematician

SOPHIE GERMAIN'S PARENTS TRIED TO KEEP HER from studying at night by putting out the fire in her room and taking away the candles. But Sophie smuggled candles in and wrapped herself in blankets. Her parents, intellectuals who were active in the French Revolution, finally left her alone.

Women could not attend the *École polytechnique* (polytechnical school) in Paris, so Sophie borrowed other students' notes and taught herself. She submitted a final paper under the name "M. LeBlanc." Impressed, the teacher, J. L. Lagrange, sought out the author. Although he was surprised that LeBlanc was a woman, he offered to guide Germain in her studies.

Germain's lack of a rigorous, traditional education handicapped her, but her progress was impressive. In 1811 the Academy of Sciences announced that a prize would be awarded to the person who provided a mathematical explanation of Ernst Chladni's experiment. The experiment involved a flat piece of metal supported horizontally and sprinkled with sand. When a violin bow was drawn along the edge, the metal vibrated, and the sand formed a pattern. After entering three times, Germain won the contest, but she didn't attend the ceremony. She felt her solution had not entirely satisfied the judges.

In 1831 Karl Gauss, one of several mathematicians who admired Germain's work and became her friend, nominated her for an honorary doctorate from the University of Göttingen in Germany. She died from cancer before receiving the degree.

Lillian Moller Gilbreth (1878–1972)
Engineer, industrial psychologist

AS THE ELDEST OF EIGHT CHILDREN, LILLIAN Moller had many responsibilities in her family's California home. After doing all her chores, though, she enjoyed studying. In 1900 she graduated at the top of her class from the University of California at Berkeley and was the school's first female commencement speaker.

Lillian met her husband, Frank Gilbreth, on a visit to Boston. Frank, a contractor, was known for combining engineering and time management to complete building projects more quickly. By 1915, when Lillian received her Ph.D. in psychology from Brown University, she had four children. Eventually the Gilbreths had twelve children, two of whom collaborated on *Cheaper by the Dozen* (1948), a book about their bustling household.

Lillian and Frank worked together to create the field of motion studies. Examining the process of work, they determined the most efficient ways to complete tasks. They set up a laboratory in their home and wrote a number of books, including *A Primer of Scientific Management* (1912).

After Frank died in 1924, Lillian began applying her expertise in motion studies to housework. She patented several inventions, including an electric mixer and a trash can with a foot pedal that opened the lid. During the 1940s she focused on making everyday tasks more convenient

for handicapped people and became a consultant to the Institute of Rehabilitation Medicine at the New York University Medical Center. Gilbreth remained active until she was over 80 years old.

Kate Gleason (1865–1933)
Engineer, builder

KATE GLEASON GREW UP WORKING WITH HER father, William, at his Rochester, New York, tool-making shop, and she continued to follow in his footsteps. In 1884 she became the first woman engineering student accepted at Cornell University. Within a year, though, financial difficulties had forced her to return to working at the family company.

In 1893, with his daughter's help, William perfected a gear-making machine that he had designed. Interestingly, many people subsequently gave Kate, rather than her father, credit for inventing the machine. It is true that she was probably responsible for its success—she had outstanding promotion and sales ability.

During World War I, Kate became acting president of the First National Bank of East Rochester. The work showed her that there was a great need for affordable housing for middle-class families. She invented a new method for pouring concrete and designed a six-room house to be built with concrete blocks. Her first housing development was "Concrest" in Rochester. It had 100 houses, each available for the reasonable price of $4,000. The project also created work for many unemployed people in the area.

Kate Gleason's housing developments became the model for many new suburbs around the country. The American Concrete Institute elected her their first woman member. When she died, her estate was worth $1.4 million, most of which was donated to charity.

Temple Grandin (1947–)
Industrial engineer

AS A CHILD, TEMPLE GRANDIN WAS DIAGNOSED with a psychological condition called autism. Social interaction is difficult for sufferers of autism, because they cannot interpret the unspoken

> "I think in pictures. Words are like a second language to me. I translate both spoken and written words into full-color movies, complete with sound, which run like a VCR tape in my head. When somebody speaks to me, his words are instantly translated into pictures. Language-based thinkers often find this phenomenon difficult to understand, but in my job as an equipment designer for the livestock industry, visual thinking is a tremendous advantage."
>
> TEMPLE GRANDIN
> *Thinking in Pictures*

emotional signals that others send. However, Temple—like many autistic people—had exceptional logic skills and high intelligence. Although doctors recommended institutionalizing the girl, her parents kept her at home in Massachusetts and sent her to private schools, where she could get the extra attention from teachers that was so necessary for her talents to be nurtured.

By 1989 Grandin had earned her Ph.D. in animal science from the University of Illinois at Urbana. She discovered that the way animals were slaughtered was a painful process that often caused the animals to panic. Using her own experiences of anxiety, she invented a humane conveyer system for handling livestock and eliminating frightening stimuli. This system is now used in over half of the cattle processing operations in America.

Many autistic people notice that applying pressure to the body helps ease anxiety. As a high school student, Grandin designed an apparatus to do this. She has since perfected the idea, creating a "squeeze machine" for use by autistic children and adults. In 1998, in collaboration with artist Wendy Jacob, she created two "squeeze chairs," which were exhibited at the Massachusetts Institute of Technology.

Dr. Grandin currently teaches at Colorado State University and consults with livestock handlers to improve their methods. Among her many publications are several books, including the memoir *Thinking in Pictures* (1995) and the technical text *Animal Welfare and Meat Science* (1999).

Evelyn Boyd Granville (1924–)
Mathematician

Evelyn Granville was raised by her mother and aunt in Washington, D.C. With scholarships and help from her family, she worked her way through Smith College and continued her studies at Yale University. Although interested in astronomy, she knew she wasn't suited to the isolation of observatory work, so she specialized in mathematics. In 1949 Granville and Marjorie Lee Browne became the first African American women to earn doctoral degrees in mathematics.

After teaching at Fisk University in Tennessee, she decided to try industrial work and accepted a job at Diamond Ordnance Fuze Laboratories in 1952. Her work there involved using mathematics to help develop fuzes, the detonating devices used to launch missiles. Later she worked for IBM on the Vanguard and Mercury space exploration probes and at the United States Space Technology Laboratories.

Returning to teaching, Granville became a faculty member at California State University in Los Angeles in 1967. She also taught math at an elementary school and directed an after-school enrichment program. In 1984 she retired to a farm in Texas, but she wasn't ready to leave the classroom. She went on to teach at Texas College and the University of Texas in Tyler. In 1989 Smith College awarded Dr. Granville the first honorary doctorate ever given to a black woman mathematician.

Mary Gray (1939–)
Mathematician, lawyer, activist

Mary Gray earned a full scholarship to Hastings College in Nebraska, where she majored in math and physics. After graduating in 1959, she studied math in Germany and then completed her Ph.D. at the University of Kansas. She began her career at American University in Washington, D.C., in 1968.

Gray became influential in mathematics education nationwide. In 1971 she was a founder and the first president of the Association for Women in Mathematics. In 1976 she became the second woman vice-president of the American Mathematical Society.

Along with her academic career, Gray has been involved in social justice issues. As a graduate student, she organized a successful protest against a grocery store that refused to hire Native Americans. She is an active member of Amnesty International, the American Civil Liberties Union, and other groups. In 1979 she received a law degree from American University. Since then she has testified before Congress several times and has advised organizations on legal issues, especially those involving women's rights and mathematics. Gray was honored in 1994 by the American Association for the Advancement of Science with their Mentor Award for Lifetime Achievement.

Catherine Littlefield Greene (1755–1814)

Patron, possible inventor

THE COTTON GIN WAS A VALUABLE AID TO SOUTHERN plantation owners, and Eli Whitney is credited with inventing it. However, Whitney had a financial backer—and, according to many historians, a collaborator—named Catherine Greene.

During the Revolutionary War, Catherine accompanied her husband, General Nathaniel Greene, on many of his assignments in George Washington's army. Afterward Washington rewarded them with a plantation in Georgia. Nathaniel died in 1786, leaving Catherine to raise their five children and run the plantation.

In 1792 Greene's plantation manager, Phineas Miller, introduced her to his friend Eli Whitney. A graduate of Yale University, Whitney enjoyed fixing mechanical items. Since he had little experience with cotton farming, it is possible that the idea of inventing a device to process cotton bolls came from Greene, as some sources suggest. Separating cotton seeds from the fibers, when done by hand, was tiresome and slow.

Greene is also said to have suggested substituting wire for wooden teeth in a part of the gin, a breakthrough that occurred after Whitney had been struggling with his invention for six months. People immediately copied the cotton gin, and Greene financed several legal battles to try to protect Whitney's claim to it. He received the patent in 1794, but only sold six machines. Greene married Phineas Miller in 1796 and later moved to a small estate in Dungeness, Georgia.

Marion Mahony Griffin (1871–1961)

Architect

ILLINOIS NATIVE MARION MAHONY STUDIED architecture at the Massachusetts Institute of Technology and in 1894 became the second woman graduate of the program. She was soon hired by famed architect Frank Lloyd Wright to work at his firm as a draftsperson. Her skillful drawings included both artistic representations of buildings and mechanical details of their construction. Her work

contributed to Wright's success. In 1898 she passed her certification exam, becoming the first woman licensed as an architect in Illinois.

In 1909 Wright left for Europe and turned his business over to Herman Von Holst, who accepted the work on condition that Mahony serve as the designer. Walter Burley Griffin, a landscape designer and architect, also joined the team. Their designs included two houses in Decatur, Illinois. Mahony's architectural style emphasized vertical lines and incorporated her love of the natural world.

In 1911 Walter and Marion were married. He established his own firm, and Marion worked as a draftsperson there, creating the drawings that brought his ideas to life. The couple worked in Australia and India until Walter's death in 1937. Marion returned to Chicago, where she opened her own practice.

Elise Harmon (1909–1985)

Mechanical and chemical engineer

ELISE HARMON MAJORED IN CHEMISTRY AT NORTH Texas State University and taught school for several years before discovering that the science she was truly "crazy about" was engineering. She went on to take graduate courses in the field at George Washington University and to work for several organizations as an engineer.

During World War II, Harmon worked with the Naval Research Laboratory in Washington, D.C. At the time American planes—unlike the more sophisticated German ones—could not fly at an altitude greater than 15,000 feet (4,572 m), the point at which the carbon brushes that were components of the planes' generators disintegrated. Harmon improved the brushes so they would function at higher altitudes. She also studied the effect of fungus on electrical equipment and performed chemical testing on materials to be used in aircraft.

In 1953 Harmon received a patent for a method of making electronic circuits in which the conducting material (silver) is printed onto the insulating material (polymerized plastic). That and her other work in "printed circuitry" contributed to the development of miniature electronic components. In 1956 Harmon was honored with the Society of Women Engineers Achievement Award. At the time of her death, she was the head of her own firm, Harmon Technical Consultants.

Lene Vestergaard Hau (1960–)
Physicist

Lene Hau was born in Denmark. A gifted student who would "rather do mathematics than go to the movies," she studied quantum mechanics at Aarhus University. She earned her Ph.D. there in 1991 and then moved to Massachusetts to work at the Rowland Institute and teach at Harvard University.

In 1994 Hau and a colleague, Dr. Jene Golovchenko, developed an apparatus they call the "candlestick," which uses lasers to cool sodium atoms to just above absolute zero (0 degrees on the Kelvin scale), a temperature so cold that it doesn't exist in nature. The super-cooled atoms almost stop moving and merge together into one superatom, forming a "Bose-Einstein condensate," a new state of matter that the physicists Satyendra Nath Bose and Albert Einstein theorized existed back in 1924.

In 1998 Hau and her research group were able to use the condensate of sodium molecules to slow the speed of light. In space, light travels at about

186,000 miles (299,330 km) per second, faster than anything else. When Hau projected a laser light beam through the condensate, though, it moved at an astonishingly slow 38 miles (61 km) per hour. There are many possible applications for the process, including glasses for night vision and optical switches for computers. Hau and her colleague Dr. Steve Harris published their findings in the February 1999 issue of the journal *Nature*.

Sophia Gregory Hayden (1868–1953)
Architect

Born in Santiago, Chile, Sophia Hayden was sent to live with her father's parents in Boston, Massachusetts, at age six. She went on to study at the Massachusetts Institute of Technology and in 1890 became the first woman to graduate from their architecture program.

Although Hayden's professors proclaimed her a brilliant student, she couldn't find work in her field. She was teaching mechanical drawing when she heard that the 1893 World's Columbian Exposition in Chicago would include a "Women's Building." There was a contest to choose the architect—and

Hayden won it. Her Italian Renaissance-style building received outstanding reviews, although some critics thought it was too feminine. She was paid a fraction of what male architects earned for designing exposition buildings.

During the exposition, rumors circulated that Hayden had experienced a nervous breakdown. It is unclear whether these rumors were true. *American Architect and Building News* used the opportunity to declare that women were not fit for architecture. Hayden's building was dismantled when the exposition closed, and she was never commissioned to build another. Around 1900 she married an artist, William Bennett, and settled in Winthrop, Massachusetts. Although Hayden was a victim of the prejudices of her time, she laid a foundation for women's success in a field that boasts thousands of female practitioners today.

Olive Clio Hazlett (1890–1974)
Mathematician

OLIVE CLIO HAZLETT EARNED HER PH.D. IN mathematics from the University of Chicago in 1915, and her doctoral dissertation was published in the *American Journal of Mathematics*. Her first teaching posts were at Bryn Mawr and Mount Holyoke colleges. Wanting more time and the resources for research, she transferred to the University of Illinois in 1924 and spent the rest of her career there. She won a prestigious Guggenheim Fellowship in 1928, which allowed her to study in Italy, Switzerland, and Germany for two years. While in Europe she attended the International Congress of Mathematicians, where she presented a paper entitled "Integers as Matrices."

Hazlett's field of expertise was algebra. She was an active member in the mathematical community. Among other positions, she served as associate editor of the *Transactions of the American Mathematical Society* from 1923 to 1935. Despite her international reputation, Hazlett was never allowed to advance beyond the position of associate professor—a fate common to many women teachers at the time—while men were promoted to full professor and allowed to teach smaller classes of more advanced students. She tried to fight the situation but with little success. The strain of this may have contributed to her battle with depression during the later part of her life.

Beulah Louise Henry (1887–after 1970)
Inventor

AS A CHILD IN TENNESSEE, BEULAH HENRY discovered that she had synesthesia, a psychological condition that causes people to experience stimuli with more senses than usual. For example, when she listened to music, Henry saw a different color for each note. Synesthesia has inspired poets and artists: Henry credited it with helping her to invent.

She received her first patent in 1912 for an ice cream freezer with a vacuum seal. Later she moved to New York City, where she tried to sell the idea of an umbrella with removable covers of different colors. Several manufacturers said that no snap was strong enough to hold the cover on in windy weather. Henry imagined an effective snap and carved it out of a bar of soap. Convinced it would work, a manufacturer paid an impressive $50,000 for the umbrella design.

Henry established a laboratory and hired mechanics to build her ideas. In 1932 she patented the "Protograph," a typewriter attachment that made an original and four copies. From 1939 to 1955, she worked as an inventor for Nicholas Machine Works. She also consulted with many firms and played a part in creating the first talking doll. Henry was so prolific and versatile that she became known as the "Lady Edison" (a reference to Thomas Edison, who invented the lightbulb). She received her 49th patent in 1970, at age 83.

Caroline Herschel (1750–1848)
Astronomer

CAROLINE HERSCHEL'S FATHER AND FOUR BROTHERS often discussed astronomy in their Hanover, Germany, home. Fascinated, she joined the conversations, although her mother disapproved. By 1772 Caroline's favorite brother, William, had moved to England to work as a musician. Soon she joined him.

Caroline worked with William as a professional singer, but after he discovered the planet Uranus, he became the court astronomer to King George III. Caroline assisted him by recording observations, doing calculations, and helping to build telescopes. Before long, they were working as a team. Together they broadened the science of astronomy from the

study of planets to the study of stars and solar systems.

In 1783 William gave Caroline her own telescope, and she began to work independently. On the night of August 1, 1786, she discovered a comet. This accomplishment had never before been credited to a woman, and it earned her a salary from the king. Over the next decade, she discovered seven more comets.

When William died in 1822, Caroline returned to Germany, where she continued working into her 90s. Scientists came from around the world to visit the famous woman astronomer. In 1835 Herschel was awarded honorary membership in the Royal Astronomical Society, along with her colleague Mary Somerville. In 1846 she received a Gold Medal for Science from the King of Prussia.

Beatrice Hicks (1919–1979)
Engineer

N EW JERSEY NATIVE BEATRICE HICKS WAS 13 years old when her father took her to New York City to see the Empire State Building and the George Washington Bridge. When he explained that engineers designed such structures, she knew that was the career she wanted. After earning her B.S. from the Newark College of Engineering, she was hired by Western Electric as a technician. Soon she was promoted to engineer.

In 1945 Hicks was hired as chief engineer for Newark Controls, her father's company. When he died the next year, she became vice-president. Her work at Newark Controls focused on designing devices to control atmospheric pressure and gas density aboard aircraft. She also continued her education, earning a master's degree in physics from Stevens Institute of Technology. By 1955 Hicks was the owner and the president of Newark Controls.

Hicks and her husband, Rodney Chipp, were actively involved with several engineering organizations. She was a founder and the first president of the Society of Women Engineers. The National Society of Professional Engineers sponsored the couple for a 1959 fact-finding trip to South America. In 1965 she became the first woman to receive an honorary doctorate from Rensselaer Polytechnic Institute.

Dorothy Hill (1907–1997)
Geologist

I N 1928 DOROTHY HILL BECAME THE FIRST WOMAN to graduate with a gold medal from Australia's University of Queensland. A geology major, she discovered her interest in ancient corals during a visit to the resort town of Mundubbera, where she found fossilized specimens from the Paleozoic era (570 million to 245 million years ago). Beginning in 1930 she spent seven years at Cambridge University in England. She compared the Mundubbera corals with British specimens of the same age and was able to correct several descriptive errors on the British ones.

In 1937 Hill returned to the University of Queensland, where she would spend the rest of her productive career. Among other activities, she and a colleague, W. H. Bryan, established a classification system for coral microstructures that is still in use. She also organized the building of a field station for scientists studying the coral reef at Heron Island.

Dr. Hill was a prolific writer, dedicated researcher, and engaging teacher. She concentrated on her research interests, never seeking fame. Her long list of firsts includes being the first woman elected a fellow of the Australian Academy of Sciences and the only woman, so far, to serve as its president.

Dorothy Crowfoot Hodgkin (1910–1994)

Chemist, X-ray crystallographer

ALTHOUGH DOROTHY CROWFOOT'S FAMILY WAS British, her father's government job took them all over the world. She attended Somerville women's college at Oxford University and earned her Ph.D. from Cambridge University. She returned to teach at Somerville in 1934, where at first she experienced discrimination because she was a woman. However, she soon won the respect of her students and colleagues. In 1937 she married historian Thomas Hodgkin, and they eventually had three children.

Dr. Hodgkin's specialty was the use of X-ray crystallography to determine a molecule's structure. The method involves exposing a crystal to an X-ray beam, which is deflected by the atoms it encounters as it passes through. The resulting pattern is imposed on photographic plates, and mathematical calculations based on the pattern reveal the molecular structure of the crystal. Hodgkin was an early user of computers to assist with the math, which was very complicated.

Between 1942 and 1945, Hodgkin determined the atomic structure of penicillin, an antibiotic. She then spent eight years determining the structure of Vitamin B_{12}, which was used to a treat a dangerous blood condition called pernicious anemia. With this information, it was possible to artificially reproduce (or synthesize) these substances. In 1964 Hodgkin won the Nobel Prize for her important discoveries. She donated the prize money for scholarships and famine relief. Even after her retirement in 1977, she traveled extensively to promote world peace.

Grace Murray Hopper (1906–1992)

Computer scientist, mathematician

TODAY WE THINK OF COMPUTERS AS SMALL DESKTOP machines. While in the navy in the 1940s, Grace Hopper worked on one that was 51 feet (16 m) long, 8 feet (2.4 m) high, and 5 feet (1.5 m) deep! Her innovations helped shrink computers so that they could be used in businesses, schools, and homes.

Hopper, a native of New York City, earned her Ph.D. in math from Yale University. After working as a professor and joining the naval reserves during World War II, she accepted a position at the Eckert-Mauchly Computer Corporation in 1949. Their computer, the UNIVAC 1 (Universal Automatic Computer), was very slow, because the user had to program in a complicated code for every calculation. Hopper created the "compiler," a tape that contained a group of programs, each assigned a call number. From then on, given the necessary call numbers, the computer could automatically carry out the programs.

Bug in the System

While Grace Murray Hopper was working on the navy's Mark 1 computer project at Harvard University, she and her team encountered a computer failure. No one could figure out what was wrong—until they opened the machine. Somehow, a moth had gotten inside, interrupting the circuits. Hopper taped the insect into her log book beside the note, "first actual bug found." Strange computer errors had been called "bugs" before, but Hopper loved telling this story and helped to make the term popular.

Dr. Hopper made computers accessible to people outside the scientific community by creating Flow-matic, the first computer language that used words instead of code. This work led to the development of COBOL (Common Business-Oriented Language), which was adopted by many businesses for data processing.

From 1967 until her retirement at age 80, Hopper was on active duty for the navy, where she eventually attained the rank of rear admiral. Her many honors include the 1991 United States Medal of Technology. The outspoken Hopper deplored resistance to change, something she had encountered often. In her office she displayed a clock that ran counterclockwise—a reminder that the unorthodox approach to a task can still be effective.

Margaret Lindsay Huggins (1848–1915)
Astronomer

DURING HER CHILDHOOD IN DUBLIN, IRELAND, Margaret Lindsay developed interests in a variety of topics, including astronomy, photography, and music. She and her grandfather viewed the constellations with homemade telescopes. She even built her own spectroscope using directions from a magazine. Margaret married astronomer William Huggins in 1875. They spent their lives together working at the Tulse Hill Observatory, near London.

Margaret used photography, a relatively new technology, to enhance their research in astronomical spectroscopy. Previously, spectroscopic images could only be recorded by written description. She experimented with several photographic methods to obtain visual records of stars' spectra. One of the pair's goals was to photograph the solar corona. They also worked to determine the chemical composition of the "chief nebular line," a certain green area in the spectra of nebulae, or areas of dust and gas in space. This research centered on comparing that line with the spectrum of burning magnesium.

Although it is clear from laboratory notes that their work was a collaboration, Margaret was not named as a coauthor on William's papers until 1889. Perhaps it took that long for them to be confident enough to challenge society's expectation that a woman would only assist her husband in his research.

Hypatia (370?–415)
Mathematician, philosopher, inventor

HYPATIA'S FATHER, THEON, WAS A MATHEMATICIAN, astronomer, and teacher at the Museum, a center for science and learning in Alexandria, Egypt. He gave his brilliant daughter the best possible education. Hypatia eventually founded her own school, and her reputation as a lecturer attracted students from around the ancient world.

All of Hypatia's writings have been lost or destroyed, but references to them remain in the letters of Synesius, one of her students. She wrote on many mathematical and astronomical topics, including a commentary on the work of Diophantus, often called the father of algebra.

Hypatia was also an inventor. Among the devices credited to her is an early astrolabe, an instrument used to calculate the positions of stars and planets. Her hydrometer, a sealed, weighted brass tube, indicated the specific gravity of a liquid by the depth to which it sank when dropped into the substance.

Hypatia lived during the rise of Christianity, and many early Christians saw science as a threat to their religion. Cyril, the patriarch of Alexandria, especially hated her. Determined to put an end to Hypatia's influence on powerful members of the government, he denounced her to a group of fanatical monks. One morning they dragged her from her carriage, then tortured and murdered her. Since then she has been famed as a martyr of the scholarly, classical world, and many consider her death the beginning of the Dark Ages in the West.

Shirley Ann Jackson (1946–)
Physicist

SHIRLEY ANN JACKSON WAS RAISED IN Washington, D.C., where she attended the accelerated mathematics and science program at Roosevelt High School. After graduating in 1964 as valedictorian, she became one of a small number of African American students at the Massachusetts Institute of Technology. She cofounded MIT's Black Student Association and served as an adviser to the university's president. In 1973 she became the first African American woman to earn a Ph.D. from MIT.

Dr. Jackson began a long career at AT&T Bell Laboratories in 1976. Her expertise in subatomic particles was important to the lab's goal of finding useful applications for materials. She worked in three different departments and published over 100 articles while at Bell Labs. She also met her husband, physicist Morris Washington, there.

In 1991 Jackson became a professor of physics at Rutgers University, and four years later she was appointed chair of the United States Nuclear Regulatory Commission. She worked hard to improve the commission's monitoring of nuclear power plants. In 1999 Jackson became president of the prestigious Rensselaer Polytechnic Institute.

Katherine Johnson (1918–)
Mathematician, aerospace technologist

THERE WEREN'T MANY EDUCATIONAL OPPORTUNITIES for African Americans in White Sulphur Springs, West Virginia, in the 1920s. To give his children a better chance, Katherine Coleman's father moved the family during the school year to the town of Institute, the home of West Virginia State College. Katherine majored in mathematics and French there and graduated *summa cum laude* (with highest honors) in 1937. Soon she married James Goble; they eventually had three children.

In 1953 Katherine began her long career at NASA's Langley Research Center in Hampton, Virginia. Her job involved using mathematical calculations to track the movement of objects in space—a complicated task that is now performed by computers. One of her projects was tracking the Earth Resource Satellite as it searched for underground minerals. During the lunar missions of the 1960s and 1970s, her calculations helped keep track of the Apollo spacecrafts. NASA recognized her work with several achievement awards.

Katherine retired in 1986. After her husband's death, she married James Johnson. In addition to working to promote better math education for children, she is also active with the Girl Scouts and the Young Women's Christian Association.

Irène Joliot-Curie (1897–1956)
Physical chemist

IRÈNE CURIE, THE DAUGHTER OF PHYSICISTS Marie and Pierre Curie, began working in her mother's laboratory at the Radium Institute in Paris in 1918. After writing a doctoral thesis on the alpha rays emitted by the radioactive element polonium, Irène received a Ph.D. from the Sorbonne in 1925. The same year Frédéric Joliot became one of Marie's assistants. Irène and Frédéric married in 1926, and both adopted the last name Joliot-Curie.

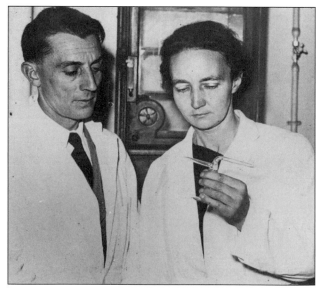

Irène Joliot-Curie with Frédéric Joliot-Curie

The couple's most famous research involved artificially creating radioactive elements by bombarding nonradioactive elements with alpha particles. For example, they exposed aluminum to alpha rays and produced radioactive isotopes of phosphorus. This work, which had important applications in medicine, earned them the 1935 Nobel Prize for chemistry.

Until the late 1930s, Irène and Frédéric always published their findings. With the rise of Nazism, however, they became concerned that their research might be misused. They stopped publishing articles and carefully hid the plans they had developed for a nuclear reactor. During World War II, they did everything they could to resist the Nazis and protect French scientists from persecution.

After the war their nuclear reactor was built. Irène became the director of the Radium Institute, and the couple continued their collaborations. Like her mother, Irène died of leukemia caused by overexposure to radiation. Seriously ill himself, Frédéric managed to carry out Irène's plans to build a nuclear physics laboratory at Orsay before his death two years later.

Amanda Theodosia Jones (1835–1914)
Inventor

AMANDA JONES'S PARENTS TAUGHT THEIR 12 children to love reading. An aspiring poet, Amanda began teaching in upstate New York at age 15 but quit when her works began to be published. She also developed a belief in the supernatural and abandoned her Methodist religion in favor of spiritualism.

The dreamy Jones had a practical side, though, and she used it to address the problem of food preservation. Traditional canning required extensive cooking. It made food less nutritious and destroyed its flavor. In her vacuum canning process, after raw food was put in jars, the air was suctioned out with valves and replaced with hot liquid just before sealing the lids. The first of Jones's nine canning patents was issued in 1872. Later, in 1890, she founded the U.S. Women's Pure Food Vacuum Preserving Company, which was almost entirely staffed by women.

Jones was living near oil fields in Pennsylvania in 1880, when she discovered that the workers had no safe way of making use of the fuel they extracted. She invented an oil burner with a valve that controlled the flow of oil. She received three patents for it and published her research in engineering magazines. Jones also continued her literary career, producing poems, stories, and a memoir, *A Psychic Autobiography* (1910).

Martine Kempf (1958–)
Inventor

GROWING UP IN STRASBOURG, FRANCE, MARTINE Kempf watched her father, a polio victim who had lost the use of his legs, make his living by inventing a car that could be controlled by the hands. She went to college in Bonn, Germany, where she met handicapped teenagers who couldn't maneuver their own wheelchairs because they had no arms. Inspired by her father, Martine decided that the answer to the problem was control by voice.

Kempf used her computer to design a program that responded to voice commands. The final product, completed in 1983, was a small box weighing under five pounds (2.3 kg). Her invention wasn't the first voice-controlled microcomputer, but it was 20 times faster than any other. She named it Katalavox, from the Greek *katal* (to understand) and the Latin *vox* (voice).

The Katalavox has been adapted for cars as well as wheelchairs. Surgeons also use it to manipulate delicate equipment during microsurgery. Among other honors, Kempf is the recipient of the 1986 Spinal Cord Society silver medal. She now lives in Sunnyvale, California, where she heads her own manufacturing and research company, KEMPF.

Margaret Knight (1838–1914)
Inventor

DESCRIBING HER CHILDHOOD IN NEW ENGLAND, Margaret Knight boasted that she made high-flying kites and that her sleds were "the envy and admiration of all the boys in town." She grew up to patent over 25 inventions and is probably responsible for many more.

Knight is said to have started her career at age 12, after witnessing an accident in a textile mill.

After a worker was hurt when a steel-tipped shuttle flew out of a loom, Knight designed a safety device to prevent such accidents.

She did not receive her first patent until she was in her 30s. Working at the Columbia Paper Bag Company in Springfield, Massachusetts, she became frustrated with the flimsy, envelope-shaped bags that were produced there. She resolved to devise something sturdier and came up with a wooden prototype machine that made the folded, flat-bottomed paper bags so familiar to modern shoppers.

Knight hired a machinist from Boston to craft the metal model of her invention that was required for a patent. A man named Charles Anning spotted it at the machinist's shop and stole the idea, obtaining the patent in his own name. Knight filed a lawsuit. She readily demonstrated her understanding of mechanics and documented her work process. The patent was granted to her in 1870. Knight went on to create inventions that benefited the shoemaking and automotive industries.

Eleanora Frances Bliss Knopf
(1883–1974)
Geologist

ELEANORA BLISS STUDIED UNDER GEOLOGIST Florence Bascom at Bryn Mawr College in her home state of Pennsylvania. After graduating in 1904, she worked as assistant curator at the college's geology museum and in the geology laboratory. In 1912 she completed her Ph.D. and began working for the United States Geological Survey (USGS).

In 1920 Eleanora married another geologist, Adolph Knopf, and moved with him to Connecticut, where he taught at Yale University. She continued to work on USGS projects. One of her most important USGS research sites was Stissing Mountain, on the border of New York and Connecticut. As part of her attempt to analyze the geological formations there and determine their origins, Eleanora went to Europe to study petrofabrics, a technique involving examination of the texture, grain, and minerals in rocks. She translated the work of the petrofabrics expert Bruno Sanders from German and introduced his methods in America.

The Knopfs lived in California after 1951, because both were offered positions at Stanford University. Eleanora was a member of several scientific organizations, including the Geological Society of America and the American Geophysical Union. Her publications include *Structural Geology* (1938) and many articles.

Sonya (Sofia) Kovalevskaia
(1850–1891)
Mathematician

IN ONE ROOM AT SOFIA KORVIN-KRUKOVSKAIA'S home in Russia, there hadn't been enough wallpaper to cover the walls, so the gaps were filled with notes from a calculus lecture. The girl loved puzzling over the numbers and symbols on the pages. A family friend who was a physics teacher noticed how brilliantly Sofia tackled the complicated subject and persuaded her parents to hire math tutors.

Sofia soon needed advanced instruction, but women weren't allowed to attend Russian universities, and her parents refused to allow her to go abroad. At age 17 she married Vladimir Kovalevski so that she could move to Germany. Although it was a marriage of convenience, Vladimir fell in love with Sofia. The couple eventually separated, but not before having a daughter.

In 1874 Kovalevskaia received a Ph.D. with highest honors from Göttingen University. Over a decade later, she was finally offered a professorship at the University of Stockholm, Sweden. While she was there she wrote a paper on the behavior of a solid rotating around a fixed point. Her complex, thorough analysis earned her the Bordin Prize from the French Academy of Sciences. The prize money was increased by 2,000 francs to acknowledge the value of her findings.

Lively and outgoing, the mathematician socialized with prominent intellectuals, including British woman novelist George Eliot. Kovalevskaia wrote poetry, fiction, and a memoir, *Recollections of Childhood* (1895). Her premature death at the age of 41 was caused by pneumonia.

Doris Kuhlmann-Wilsdorf (1922–)
Metallurgist

BORN IN BREMEN, GERMANY, DORIS KUHLMANN earned her Ph.D. in 1947 from Göttingen University, where she studied physics, chemistry, and mathematics. She married Heinz Wilsdorf three years later. After teaching and studying in England and South Africa, she went to the United States to teach in the metallurgical engineering department at the University of Pennsylvania. In 1963 she began working at the University of Virginia. She has been a consultant to government agencies and to corporations such as General Dynamics.

Dr. Kuhlmann-Wilsdorf's research has focused on the structure, properties, and uses of metals. She has studied the plastic deformation of solids, or the inability of some materials to resume their original shapes after being subjected to stress. One of her most important achievements has been designing metal-fiber brushes for use in electric motors. The navy hopes to use them to improve the function of their ships. She holds three patents for her inventions.

Kuhlmann-Wilsdorf is also interested in the relationship between science and religion. She feels that modern science, especially quantum mechanics, is quite compatible with spiritual beliefs. She has been recognized for her work with many honors, including the Society of Women Engineers Achievement Award in 1989.

Stephanie Louise Kwolek (1923–)
Chemist, inventor

STEPHANIE KWOLEK ATTENDED THE CARNEGIE Institute of Technology in her home state of Pennsylvania. After graduating in 1946, she began working at the DuPont Company labs, intending to stay just long enough to earn tuition for medical school. In 1950 DuPont moved their Pioneering Research Laboratory to Wilmington, Delaware, and Kwolek, too fascinated with her work to bother with medical school, went with them.

Kwolek's most famous discovery resulted from her work making synthetic fibers out of polymers (compounds that consist of repeating structural units). She moved from one advance to the next and eventually developed Kevlar, which was released by DuPont in 1971. Lightweight yet many times stronger than steel, it is used to make bulletproof vests and has numerous other applications, from fire-protective clothing to extra-strong cables to airplane and automobile construction.

As a woman scientist, Kwolek often experienced discrimination, but that didn't hamper her productivity. DuPont delayed her promotions, at least until Kevlar proved to be an extremely lucrative product. In order to be taken seriously in her field, she often signed her publications "S. L. Kwolek." She holds seven patents in her own name and shares nine with other scientists. Along with many other awards, she was inducted into the National Inventors Hall of Fame in 1995. She retired in 1986 but continues to consult for E. I. DuPont de Nemours and Company.

Christine Ladd-Franklin (1847–1930)
Logician, psychologist

CHRISTINE LADD'S MOTHER DIED AROUND 1859, and afterward she lived in New Hampshire with her grandmother. She majored in mathematics at Vassar College and then taught school for several years and wrote math articles for *The Educational Times*. With the support of Professor James Sylvester, she enrolled at Johns Hopkins University in Baltimore as a special graduate student. She completed the requirements for a Ph.D. in 1878 but, as a woman, was not eligible for the degree. In 1882 she married Fabian Franklin, a mathematics professor at Johns Hopkins.

Ladd-Franklin was interested in symbolic logic, a science that uses mathematical principles to study the reasoning process. She devised a way of testing logical deductions through "antilogisms," which were made up of three incompatible statements. Later she became interested in color vision. In 1891 she traveled to Germany, where she worked with two vision experts. Her conclusion that the ability to distinguish different colors evolved gradually from sensitivity to light, or the color white, became the accepted theory of color vision for many years.

Ladd-Franklin worked hard to bring more women into scientific institutions, both as students and professors. In addition to publishing such scholarly works as *Colour and Colour Theories* (1929), she enjoyed writing opinionated letters to the editor of the *New York Times*. In 1926 Johns Hopkins awarded her the Ph.D. she had earned 48 years earlier.

Hedy Lamarr (1913–2000)
Inventor, actress

Hedy Lamarr was a glamorous movie actress during the 1940s—no one suspected at the time that she was also an inventor. As Hedwig Kiesler of Vienna, Austria, she had been married to a weapons dealer. He and his friends often discussed

communication technology, and she paid careful attention. Later she left him and began her Hollywood career under her new name.

In 1941, with World War II in progress, Lamarr and George Antheil, a composer, received patent #2,292,387 for a communication system. This technology allowed for radio messages to change frequencies during broadcast. A specially designed receiver was needed to intercept the messages. Lamarr and Antheil gave the patent rights to the United States government, but, as it turned out, the system wasn't used during the war. It remained classified information until the 1980s. Today "spread spectrum" technology is used to make more radio waves available to cellular phones and other modern communication systems.

For over 50 years, Lamarr denied rumors of her technological abilities, but in 1997 she acknowledged her part in the invention. That year she and Antheil received an Electric Frontier Foundation Pioneer Award and were honored at the 11th annual Invention Convention.

Bertha Lamme (1869–1954)
Engineer

As a girl Bertha Lamme was known as the brightest, most dedicated student in her class. She went on to attend Ohio State University, where her older brother, Benjamin, was already a student. Benjamin was a strong influence on his sister. When Bertha fell ill during her senior year, he tutored her so that she could graduate on time. In 1893 she became the second woman in the United States—and the first at Ohio State—to earn a degree in engineering.

Bertha joined Benjamin in working at Westinghouse Electric and Manufacturing Company in Pittsburgh, Pennsylvania. There she became a member of an engineering team designing motors and generators. In 1905 she married her supervisor, Russell Feicht.

Like so many women scientists of the time, Bertha cut her career short after marrying. Westinghouse records indicate that she performed exceptionally well as a design engineer, but little specific documentation of her work has survived. She undoubtedly contributed to the engineering projects of her brother and husband, who both designed generators, an area of expertise for her. She may also have inspired her daughter, Florence, who eventually became a physicist.

Marie Anne Pierrette Paulze Lavoisier (1758–1836)

Chemist, scientific illustrator

MARIE PAULZE WAS 14 YEARS OLD WHEN SHE married Antoine Laurent Lavoisier, a chemist and member of the French Academy of Sciences. From then on, Marie shared in all of Antoine's endeavors. She learned to read Latin and English, kept the laboratory records, and maintained their correspondence with other scientists. Intellectuals from around the world visited them to socialize and discuss their work.

Marie helped Antoine change one of the basic assumptions about chemistry. Most scientists then believed that anything flammable contained a material called phlogiston, which was depleted during the act of burning. However, the Lavoisiers' experiments showed that combustion resulted from the combination of a burning material with something in the air. They worked further to isolate that gas, and Antoine named it oxygen. His subsequent book, *Elements of Chemistry* (1789), for which Marie created the illustrations, is considered the first modern chemistry text.

> "Madame Lavoisier, a lively, sensible, scientific lady, had prepared a déjeuner Anglois [English luncheon] of tea and coffee, but her conversation on Mr. Kirwan's Essay on Phlogiston, which she is translating from the English, and on other subjects, which a woman of understanding that works with her husband in his laboratory knows how to adorn, was the best repast."
>
> **British writer ARTHUR YOUNG after visiting the Lavoisiers**

As members of the aristocracy, the Lavoisiers came under attack during the French Revolution. Antoine was executed in 1794, and Marie was briefly imprisoned. Afterward she edited and completed her husband's eight-volume work, *Mémoires de chimie* (1805, Memoirs on chemistry). Her second marriage to the physicist Benjamin Thompson, Count Rumford, lasted only four years. Marie's home remained a popular gathering place for scientists until her death.

Henrietta Swan Leavitt (1868–1921)

Astronomer

A DESCENDANT OF THE PURITANS, MASSACHUSETTS native Henrietta Leavitt was a senior at the Society for the Collegiate Instruction of Women (later Radcliffe College) when she took her first astronomy course. Fascinated, she stayed an extra year to learn more about it. Leavitt, who had suffered severe hearing loss because of an illness, was a brilliant student. In 1895 she began volunteering at the Harvard College Observatory, and by 1902 she was a full-time employee.

Leavitt was chosen to lead a project on determining the magnitude, or brightness, of stars. She concentrated on a group of 46 stars, using 299 photographs taken through 13 telescopes to establish standard values of magnitude that could be applied to other stars. In 1913 the International Committee on Photographic Magnitudes adopted her system for mapping the entire sky.

She also contributed to the study of variable stars. Certain variable stars, the Cepheid class, pulsate in a regular pattern. She determined that the longer a Cepheid star took to go from brightness to dimness, the brighter it actually was. This later helped astronomers determine many stars' distance from Earth.

Leavitt was considered one of the observatory's smartest astronomers, no small accomplishment for someone whose colleagues were Annie Jump Cannon, Antonia Maury, and Williamina Fleming. But at the time women weren't encouraged to develop their own theories. Therefore, Leavitt dedicated herself to the essential background research that advanced the work of others.

Désirée Le Beau (1907–1993)
Chemist

Désirée Le Beau discovered chemistry by accident. A native of Teschen, Austria-Hungary (now Poland), she attended college at the University of Vienna in Austria. One day she went to the chemistry laboratory, mistakenly thinking it was her class in pharmacology (the study of medical drugs). She liked chemistry so much that she decided to stay. In 1931 she earned a Ph.D. in chemistry from the University of Graz. She worked in Vienna and

Paris until 1936, when she became a research chemist for Dewey and Almy Company in Massachusetts.

Le Beau's field of expertise was rubber reclamation, or recycling. As World War II gripped Europe, rubber supplies were limited, and her research into the properties of both synthetic and natural rubber helped keep these useful materials available. By 1945 she had become the director of research at the Midwest Rubber Reclaiming Company in Illinois.

Le Beau earned patents for several of her innovations, which included a process for making padding for railroad ties from recycled rubber. She was a fellow of the American Institute of Chemists, and in 1959 the Society of Women Engineers honored her with their annual Achievement Award.

Inge Lehmann (1888–1993)
Seismologist

As a child in Copenhagen, Inge Lehmann attended a progressive coeducational school that fostered her interest in science. She eventually earned a master's degree in mathematics at the University of Copenhagen. She was an assistant at the Royal Danish Geodetic Institute in 1925, when a shipment of seismographs arrived. Lehmann was fascinated by the machines, which are used to record vibrations in the ground. Her boss arranged for her to study for five months in Germany with seismologist Beno Gutenberg. By 1928 she had become chief of the institute.

Lehmann began corresponding with the British seismologist Harold Jeffreys, who theorized that the center of the Earth was made entirely of molten rock. Early evidence supported this idea, and most scientists came to agree with him. But as Lehmann studied the seismic records of Pacific earthquakes, it became apparent to her that the Earth must have a solid center surrounded by a layer of molten rock.

Lehmann's paper explaining her findings, "P-prime" (1936), shocked seismologists at first, but they soon realized she was correct. The difference in the materials that make up the Earth's core is now called the "Lehmann discontinuity." Lehmann received many honors during her long career, including the 1971 William Bowie Medal, awarded by the American Geophysical Union.

Halley's Comet

In 1705 the astronomer Edmond Halley theorized that comets seen in 1531, 1607, and 1682 were actually only one comet, which would return in 1758 (it was visible again in early 1759). Halley died in 1742, but Nicole Lepaute and Alexis Clairant confirmed his prediction and named the comet after him. Comets are made up of dust and ice. They are only visible from Earth when they circle near the sun, at which point many form long tails, as dust particles are expelled from the nucleus by escaping gases. Halley's Comet is visible every 76 years or so and is predicted to reappear in 2061.

Nicole-Reine Étable de la Brière Lepaute (1723–1788)

Astronomer

NICOLE-REINE ÉTABLE DE LA BRIÈRE GREW UP IN aristocratic surroundings at the Luxembourg Palace in Paris. She became interested in astronomy and mathematics while working with her husband, Jean André Lepaute, the clockmaker to the king, and performed important calculations for his book, *Traité d'horlogerie* (1755, Treatise on clockmaking).

The Paris Observatory hired Nicole and mathematician Alexis Clairant in 1757 to predict exactly when Halley's Comet would return in 1759. The calculations were difficult, because they had to consider the gravitational pull of Jupiter and Saturn. The pair were successful, but Clairant is usually given sole credit for the work.

From 1760 to 1776, Lepaute worked with astronomer Joseph Lalande to produce the Academy of Sciences' annual almanac. It included tables that listed the locations of the sun, moon, planets, and stars for every day of the year. This information was essential to navigators of ships, who used the book to plan their journeys. Failing eyesight finally forced Lepaute into retirement, and she died at age 65.

Leona Woods Marshall Libby (1919–1986)

Physicist

ALTHOUGH LEONA WOODS'S FAMILY STRUGGLED financially during the Great Depression, the five children were expected to go to college. Leona earned a scholarship and worked part-time so she could study chemistry at the University of Chicago, not far from her family home. She graduated early, at age 19.

While Woods was working toward her Ph.D., she was involved with the construction of the first nuclear fission reactor, the Chicago Pile 1 (CP-1). The project, code-named Chicago Metallurgical Laboratory, was led by Nobel prizewinner Enrico Fermi, an important mentor to Woods and other women physicists. She was the only woman to witness the first nuclear chain reaction in 1942.

Woods spent her career combining teaching positions with research opportunities. For example, she worked as a consultant to Rand Corporation analyzing national defense issues and also taught at the University of Chicago. Her first marriage, to physicist John Marshall, Jr., ended in divorce. She and her second husband, Willard Libby, helped establish the Environmental Science and Engineering Department at the University of California at Los Angeles. Leona Libby wrote several books, including *The Uranium People* (1979), and many articles.

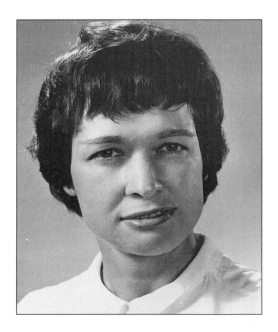

Dame Kathleen Lonsdale (1903–1971)

Physicist, chemist, X-ray crystallographer

IN 1922 KATHLEEN YARDLEY GRADUATED WITH A degree in physics from Bedford College in London, having earned the highest marks of any student during the preceding decade. Nobel prize-winner W. H. Bragg invited her to work at his laboratory, using X-ray analysis to determine the structure of organic molecules.

In 1927 Kathleen married a colleague, Thomas Lonsdale, and they moved to Leeds. She continued the work she had begun with Bragg at the university there. Her important discovery that the molecule hexamethylbenzene had a hexagonal, flat shape was enthusiastically supported by Bragg, even though he had predicted that the molecule would be puckered.

After returning to London, Lonsdale earned her Ph.D. in 1934 and resumed working with Bragg at the Royal Institution. In 1945 she and microbiologist Marjory Stephenson became the first female fellows of the Royal Society. Four years later Lonsdale became the first woman professor at University College in London. She was declared a Dame of the British Empire in 1956.

In addition to her scientific career, Lonsdale was active in the pacifist, prison reform, and antinuclear movements. The Lonsdales had adopted the Quaker religion in 1936, shortly after the birth of their third child. They sheltered refugees during World War II, and Dame Kathleen spent time in jail for refusing to perform civil defense duties. Later she traveled around the world, lecturing about her beliefs.

Augusta Ada Byron, Countess of Lovelace (1815–1852)

Mathematician

COMPUTERS ARE A MODERN INVENTION, BUT they have their roots in the 19th-century work of Ada Byron, Countess of Lovelace. Ada was the daughter of the English poet George Gordon, Lord Byron, but she never met him. Raised by her mother, she was encouraged to study mathematics and science. She corresponded with the mathematician Mary Somerville and had influential scientists as tutors.

In 1833 Ada met Charles Babbage and became fascinated with his invention, the "Analytical Engine." This machine, operated by cranks and gears, could compute and print out mathematical tables. When an Italian scientist published an article on Babbage's invention, Ada translated it. Then, with Babbage's encouragement, she added twice as much new information. Soon they were working together on improving his "calculating engine."

Babbage's original machine was based on a decimal system of numbers. Engaging in the earliest form of "computer programming," Byron developed a binary system, in which everything was represented by ones and zeroes, so that their "computer" could solve more complicated problems. She even wrote an article predicting that someday this machine would be able to create graphics and write music.

Byron married William, Count Lovelace, in 1835 and bore three children. She experienced many personal problems, including poor health and an addiction to gambling. Those difficulties and her early death at age 36 from cancer have led some scholars to question the degree of her involvement in Babbage's work. Recent biographical research, however, has affirmed the importance of her contribution.

Shannon Lucid (1943–)
Astronaut, biochemist

GROWING UP IN OKLAHOMA, SHANNON LUCID dreamed of being an explorer in the American West. She ended up exploring outer space. She earned her undergraduate degree in chemistry and her Ph.D. in biochemistry at the University of Oklahoma. Until 1978, when she was accepted into NASA's astronaut training program, Lucid worked as a teacher and researcher.

After qualifying as an astronaut, Lucid spent six years as a mission control specialist. Her responsibilities included payload testing, launch countdowns, and communication with space shuttles. On June 17, 1985, she made her first spaceflight aboard the shuttle *Discovery*, where she performed biochemistry experiments and deployed satellites.

In 1989 Lucid performed a five-day mission on the shuttle *Atlantis*. One of the crew's goals was deploying the *Galileo*, a spacecraft bound for Jupiter. She worked on the *Atlantis* again in 1991, orbiting Earth 142 times during the nine-day mission. In 1993 on the *Columbia*, Lucid and her fellow crew members achieved a record-length mission of 14 days, during which they used themselves as subjects for physiology experiments and performed engineering tests.

Lucid traveled aboard *Atlantis* to join two cosmonauts at the Russian space station *Mir* in 1996. Her mission lasted a total of 188 days, which broke the record for the longest stay in space by an American astronaut.

Elsie Gregory MacGill (1908–1980)
Aeronautical engineer

THERE WAS A TRADITION OF STRONG, INDEPENDENT women in Elsie MacGill's Canadian family. Her grandmother was active in the suffrage movement, and her mother was a judge. MacGill attended the University of Toronto and in 1927 became the institution's first woman student to receive a bachelor's degree in electrical engineering.

MacGill moved to the United States to work for Austin Aircraft Company while she attended graduate school in aeronautical engineering at the University of Michigan. Even after contracting polio, she refused to put off receiving her master's degree—she took her final exams at the hospital. MacGill soon regained her ability to walk. In 1937 she was hired by the Canadian Car and Foundry Company as chief aeronautical engineer. She became the first woman to design, build, and test an airplane when she led the construction of the *Maple Leaf II* for the Mexican Air Force.

During World War II, MacGill converted a railroad boxcar plant into a factory to produce Hawker Hurricane fighter planes for Great Britain. By 1941 she had nearly 5,000 employees—many of them women—turning out 23 planes each week. After the war MacGill continued her career in engineering and her advocacy for working women.

Jane Haldimand Marcet (1769–1858)
Science writer

JANE HALDIMAND GREW UP IN LONDON AS THE daughter of a prosperous Swiss merchant. In 1799 she married Alexander Marcet, a physician and chemist. Soon Jane, too, became interested in chemistry. She began attending lectures, especially those by Sir Humphry Davy, a popular speaker at the Royal Institution.

Marcet found it easier to follow the lectures if she discussed the topics with others beforehand. She used this idea to write *Conversations on Chemistry* (1806), a book featuring a chemistry teacher and her two students. Attempting to capture the attention of the less interested student, the teacher performs several experiments. The book, which also included illustrations by Marcet, quickly became popular. It went through 16 British editions and sold well in America, France, and Germany.

Although Jane Marcet's book influenced many people, its most famous reader was probably chemist Michael Faraday, who read it when he was 13 years old. Marcet and Faraday became friends, and she always consulted him when editing new editions. She went on to publish several other works, including *Conversations on Political Economy* (1816).

Maria Prophetissa (1st or 2nd century)

Alchemist, inventor

MARIA PROPHETISSA, ALSO CALLED MARY THE Jewess or Miriam, was an alchemist in ancient Alexandria, Egypt. One of the goals of alchemy was transforming common metals into gold or silver. Although that proved impossible, alchemists were the first to use experiments to test their theories. Maria made significant contributions to science by inventing laboratory tools.

The *balneum mariae* (Maria's bath) is a water bath used to heat substances slowly or keep them at a constant temperature. The double boiler, a common cooking utensil, is essentially a *balneum mariae*; in France it is called a *bain-marie*. Maria also invented the *tribikos*, or three-part still, which is used to heat three liquids, combine their vapors, and then cool the blended vapors so that they condense into a fourth liquid.

Maria's experiments with the effect of arsenic, mercury, and sulfur vapors on metal alloys led her to devise the *kerotakis* (heated pallet), a cylinder with a sealed top and a flame at the bottom. Close to the top, the metal rests on a pallet, or small platform; the element to be vaporized is suspended over the fire. The vapor reacts with the alloy and then resolidifies into a compound. Using this apparatus, Maria created a black sulfide that modern chemists still call "Mary's Black."

Sybilla Masters (1671?–1720)

Inventor

ALTHOUGH HANNAH SLATER RECEIVED THE FIRST U.S. patent granted to a woman in 1793 (under the name Mrs. Samuel Slater), a colonial woman, Sybilla Masters, received credit for two inventions decades before the American Revolution. Little is known about Sybilla's early life. A Quaker, she married Thomas Masters in the 1690s, and they settled in Philadelphia. They had four children who survived infancy. Thomas, a wealthy landowner, became mayor of Philadelphia and, later, a provincial councillor.

Sybilla's first invention was a device for processing corn by crushing the grain rather than grinding it, as was the traditional method. In 1712 she went to London, England, and secured patent #401 for the apparatus. The patent was issued in her husband's name, but it credited Sybilla as the inventor.

Four years later she received patent #403 for a fiber-making and staining process that used straw and palmetto tree leaves to create hats and other items. Thomas was granted a monopoly on importing palmetto leaves from the West Indies. For a year Sybilla sold her fiber products from a shop in London. Then she and her husband returned to Philadelphia, where Sybilla's patents were recognized by the Provincial Council.

Antonia Caetana Maury (1866–1952)

Astronomer

ANTONIA MAURY CAME FROM AN EDUCATED NEW York family. Her uncle was Henry Draper, a gifted amateur astronomer. After she graduated from Vassar College, she went to work at the Harvard College Observatory. There she participated in the Henry Draper Memorial Project, funded by her aunt, Mary Draper.

The focus of the Draper Project was on classifying stars using spectroscopy, photographing the stars through a telescope with a prism in front of its lens. The process revealed the stars' characteristic spectra. The project employed many important women astronomers. Although they had no freedom to develop their own theories, most were pleased to be able to work in their field.

However, as Maury studied the photographic plates, she formulated her own, more detailed, classification system. Edward Pickering, the director of the observatory, wanted her to stick with his system. They argued often, and after 1892 Maury devoted herself to teaching. Five years later, however, she published an article about her system in the *Annals of the Harvard College Observatory*.

In 1905 Ejnar Hertzsprung, an influential Danish astronomer, used Maury's system to further his research. He wrote to Pickering praising Maury's work, but that didn't change Pickering's opinion. Maury returned to the observatory in 1918, and by 1920 there was a new director, Harlow Shapley, who allowed her greater freedom. During these later years, she studied binary stars (paired stars that revolve around each other). In 1943 she was awarded the Annie J. Cannon Prize for astronomy.

Maria Gertrude Goeppert Mayer (1906–1972)
Physicist, mathematician

MARIA GOEPPERT SPENT HER CHILDHOOD IN Göttingen, Germany, where her father was a medical professor. In 1930, after writing a highly acclaimed dissertation and receiving her Ph.D. in physics, she married Joseph Mayer, an American physicist. They moved to Baltimore, where Joseph had won a position at Johns Hopkins University.

The Nuclear Shell Model

The nucleus, or central region of the atom, is made up of protons and neutrons. When Mayer began studying the structure of the nucleus, she noticed that atoms of certain especially stable (nonreactive) elements contained specific even numbers of protons or neutrons. The physicist Enrico Fermi had suggested that the particles might be paired (proton with proton and neutron with neutron) and spinning in separate spherical layers within the nucleus. Mayer agreed and, using math, was able to support the theory. Because she compared the layers of protons and neutrons to shells, this idea is called the nuclear shell model.

Much of Maria's teaching and research was done without pay, because she was not allowed to have an official position at the same university as her husband. Despite that and the fact that she raised two children, she remained devoted to her work. In 1940 she and Joseph published a textbook, *Statistical Mechanics*, which is now a classic. She also worked on the Manhattan Project at Columbia University, performing secret research toward the development of the atomic bomb.

In 1946 the Mayers went to work at the University of Chicago, where Maria researched the structure of the atom's nucleus. Both Maria and another scientist, Hans Jensen, published articles reporting the same findings in 1949. She and Jensen went on to coauthor *Elementary Theory of Nuclear Shell Structure* (1955), and in 1963 they shared the Nobel Prize in physics with Eugene Wigner.

Lise Meitner (1878–1968)
Physicist

LISE MEITNER WAS BORN TO A JEWISH FAMILY IN Vienna, Austria. Although her formal schooling had ended at age 14, she convinced her parents to let her take the college entrance examinations. She

was one of only a few women admitted to the University of Vienna, where she studied until receiving a Ph.D. in physics in 1906.

In 1907 she moved to Berlin, where she met many important scientists, including Max Planck and Otto Hahn. Meitner and Hahn became a great scientific team. They discovered a new element, protactinium, in 1917. They were studying the nucleus of the atom when the rise of Nazism forced Meitner to flee to Sweden in 1938. She was hired by the Nobel Institute for Physics and continued to correspond with Hahn.

Hahn and Meitner had been bombarding uranium with neutrons, and Hahn determined that this had created barium, but he could not explain why. Repeating the experiments, Meitner and her nephew, Otto Frisch, realized that they were splitting the uranium atom, a process Meitner called "nuclear fission." She knew that, under the proper conditions, an enormous amount of energy would be released as the nucleus shattered, and she published that information in 1939. It proved central in the creation of the atomic bomb. Meitner, a pacifist, was always deeply disturbed that her research had been used so destructively.

In 1966 Meitner received the Enrico Fermi Award for her contribution to science. Element number 109, meitnerium, was discovered and named after her in 1994.

Maria Mitchell (1818–1889)
Astronomer

MARIA MITCHELL GREW UP IN NANTUCKET, Massachusetts, a whaling town populated by seamen whose lives depended on understanding the stars. She and her father spent many evenings together observing the skies through a telescope. Although Maria's formal schooling ended at age 16, she educated herself about astronomy by reading books at the Nantucket Library, where she worked, and attending lectures.

On the night of October 1, 1847, Mitchell saw a faint light in the sky above the star Polaris. She knew it had not been there before and realized it was a comet. When her discovery was confirmed in 1848, Mitchell was awarded a gold medal by King Frederick VII of Denmark. She traveled to Europe, where she was thrilled to meet the mathematician Mary Somerville. Soon afterward she became the first woman elected to the American Association for the Advancement of Science.

In 1865 Vassar College, a women's educational institution, was founded in Poughkeepsie, New York. Mitchell's prestige made her the ideal candidate for teaching there. Having never attended college, she worried that she might not be qualified but finally accepted the positions of professor of astronomy and director of the observatory and retained them until the year before her death.

Although Mitchell continued her astronomical research, her greatest contribution may have been her ability to inspire students. Insisting that they learn by observation and experience, she avoided textbooks and lecturing except on the subject of mathematics, which she felt was a foundation of astronomy. An advocate for women's rights, she helped found the Association for the Advancement of Women in 1873.

Ann Moore (1940–)
Inventor

DURING THE 1960s ANN MOORE AND HER husband, Mike, joined the Peace Corps. While working as a nurse in Togo, Africa, Ann noticed mothers carrying their babies on their backs in cloth slings. After returning home to Colorado, she gave birth to a daughter and improvised a carrier of her own from a piece of fabric. She described the idea to her mother, Lucy Aukerman, who was a skilled seamstress. Aukerman attached zippers and straps to a sheet and created the first "Snugli."

The Moores used the Snugli all the time, even while taking part in Martin Luther King's 1965 civil rights march from Selma to Montgomery, Alabama. Many people asked to buy one. The Moores and Aukerman patented the design the next year and by 1972 had formed a corporation. In 1985 they sold the company to the Huffy Corporation.

The next year a medical worker named Leslie Beauparlant asked Ann to help design a carrier for personal medical equipment, especially portable oxygen tanks. She came up with a lightweight, comfortable backpack that was much more convenient for patients than the traditional cart. The Moores' new company, which they formed with Beauparlant, is called Airlift Unlimited.

Julia Morgan (1872–1957)
Architect

JULIA MORGAN, AN ARCHITECT WHO DESIGNED OVER 700 buildings, achieved many firsts in her lifetime. She was the first woman admitted to study engineering at the University of California at Berkeley. She attended the École des Beaux-Arts in Paris and in 1902 became the first woman to graduate from there. Soon afterward she received the first architect's license ever awarded to a woman in California, her home state.

Morgan started her career with the architect John Galen Howard. Although she worked on interesting projects, such as a theater and a building to house the mining department at the university in Berkeley, she became frustrated with her low pay and poor treatment by male colleagues. She opened her own office in San Francisco in 1904 and made a point of hiring many women to work there. One of her most prestigious commissions was redesigning the Fairmont Hotel, which had been damaged in the San Francisco fire of 1906. She also designed homes in the San Francisco area and buildings on the Berkeley campus.

Morgan had a long relationship with the Hearst family, most notably with Phoebe Hearst and her son, William Randolph. She designed a castle and guest houses for William at San Simeon, as well as buildings for his newspaper business in San Francisco and Los Angeles. Outside of work she lived a quiet life, socializing mainly with her family. She retired in 1946.

Nitokris (around 7th century B.C.E.)
Builder, queen

THE HISTORIAN HERODOTUS WRITES OF A QUEEN named Nitokris, who was famed for her building projects in ancient Assyria. It is no longer known exactly who she was. Some present-day historians identify her as Naqi'a, wife of the powerful king Sennacherib, who reigned from 704 to 681 B.C.E. Others believe she was Addagoppe, wife of the ruler Labynetus, who flourished a few decades later. If she was Addagoppe, contemporary accounts suggest that she lived to the remarkable age of 104 and died around 547 B.C.E.

Nitokris was said to have been responsible for directing the rebuilding of Babylon after it was destroyed by a flood. Both Herodotus, writing in the fifth century B.C.E., and another historian, Diodorus Siculus, writing about 400 years later, mention the monumental achievements of Nitokris/Naqi'a. These included a reservoir, a temple, an ingenious removable bridge across the Euphrates River, and two palaces connected by a tunnel underneath the river.

Ida Tacke Noddack (1896–1979)
Chemist

AFTER EARNING HER DOCTORATE FROM THE University of Berlin, Ida Tacke began working at the Physio-Technical Research Agency with her future husband, Walter Noddack. Their research was focused on finding elements number 43 and 75 in the incomplete periodic table of elements. In 1925 they isolated number 75 from molybdenite ore. They named it rhenium after the Rhine, a major German river.

Ida's next research was related to physicist Enrico Fermi's experiments in bombarding uranium with neutrons. He and others thought this process was creating completely new elements. Ida disagreed,

The Periodic Table

Russian chemist Dmitry Mendeleyev published the first periodic table of the elements in 1869. He started by making a card for each known element, noting the element's symbol and atomic weight. Then, as if he were playing solitaire, he arranged the cards in order of increasing atomic weight, grouping those with similar chemical and physical properties in rows, or periods. If a sequence was incomplete, Mendeleyev predicted (correctly) that the gaps would be filled as more elements were discovered. Small changes have since been made to the table, and new elements, such as Ida Noddack's rhenium, have been added, but Mendeleyev's classification system still holds.

theorizing that the nucleus of the uranium atom was being split, causing isotopes of already known elements to be formed. At the time she was ignored, but five years later, Lise Meitner and two other scientists produced evidence that proved Noddack right. The process was named nuclear fission.

The Noddacks worked together at the universities in Freiburg and Strasbourg, then at the State Research Institute for Geochemistry in Bamberg until Walter's death in 1960. Among many other honors, Ida received the High Service Cross of the German Federal Republic in 1966. She retired to Bad Neuenahr, a town on the Rhine, two years later.

Amalie (Emmy) Noether (1882–1935)
Mathematician

EINSTEIN CALLED EMMY NOETHER A "CREATIVE, mathematical genius," and her revolutionary contributions to the field of abstract algebra changed the way everyone looked at math. Yet, because she was a woman, she spent most of her career without a paid teaching job.

Emmy Noether belonged to an intellectual German Jewish family. Her father was a math professor at the University of Erlangen, and her mother was a musician. When she decided to go to college to study math, women weren't allowed to receive degrees from German universities. From 1900 to 1903, she audited courses (that is, attended them without receiving formal credit) at Erlangen. She then spent a semester studying in Göttingen and returned to Erlangen after the school decided to admit women.

In 1907 Noether received her Ph.D., graduating with highest honors. Because her father was in poor health, she began teaching many of his classes, unofficially and without pay. In 1914 she went to work with mathematician David Hilbert at the University of Göttingen. Among her projects was collaborating with Hilbert on developing the mathematical formulas to support Albert Einstein's theory of relativity. Noether had started out unpaid at the university, but by the 1920s she was receiving a small salary.

In 1933, when Hitler came to power, Noether and her other Jewish colleagues were fired. Leaving Germany, she accepted a position at Bryn Mawr College in Pennsylvania. Her sudden death was caused by an infection following surgery.

Adriana Ocampo (1955–)
Planetary geologist

WHEN SHE WAS A CHILD IN Argentina, Adriana Ocampo pretended that her dolls were astronauts and the kitchen appliances were spaceships. Her family immigrated to the United States when she was 15 years old. While she was still in high school in Pasadena, California, Adriana took a summer job at NASA's Jet Propulsion Laboratory (JPL). She continued working there part-time while earning her bachelor's degree in geology and accepted a full-time post after graduating in 1983.

Ocampo has participated in numerous NASA projects. After analyzing images from the Viking mission to Mars, she compiled a photo atlas of the Martian moon, Phobos, in 1984. She contributed to the Project Galileo mission to Jupiter by directing the operation of a device aboard the unmanned spacecraft that measured reflected sunlight in Jupiter's atmosphere.

Fluent in Spanish and English, Ocampo makes many public appearances and works to promote communication among scientists. She helped organize a Pan-American space conference, which was held in Costa Rica in 1990, Chile in 1993, and Uruguay in 1996. She is also a member of the Chicxulub Consortium, which studies a crater formed in Mexico when an asteroid struck the Earth about 65 million years ago. That collision is believed to have led to the extinction of the dinosaurs. Ocampo has been married since 1989 to archaeologist Kevin Pope.

Ellen Ochoa (1958–)
Electrical engineer, astronaut

ELLEN OCHOA, WHO GREW UP IN A CHICANO family in southern California, was always interested in a wide variety of subjects. In 1976 she started as a music major at San Diego State University, and then she changed her focus to physics. She went on to earn a Ph.D. in electrical engineering from Stanford University.

Ochoa began working at Sandia National Laboratories in 1985. Her research there focused on improving imaging technology, and she obtained three patents for inventions in that field. In 1988 she accepted a position at NASA's Ames Research Center. Ochoa was soon supervising a team of 35 scientists in the center's Intelligent Systems Technology Branch. In 1990 she was chosen for astronaut training—she would become the first Mexican American woman in space.

On April 8, 1993, space shuttle *Discovery* took off with Ochoa and four other astronauts onboard. Ochoa performed research on variations in the sun's activity and how that affected Earth's atmosphere. She was also responsible for deploying and capturing the *Spartan* satellite. Ochoa also flew on space missions in November 1994 and May 1999. She has never abandoned her love for music and continues to play the flute. Her honors include the 1993 Congressional Hispanic Caucus Medallion of Excellence Role Model Award.

Ida Ogilvie (1874–1963)
Geologist

IDA OGILVIE'S WEALTHY NEW YORK CITY FAMILY expected her to marry and have children. Instead she attended Bryn Mawr College, where she studied geology with Florence Bascom. She began her graduate studies at the University of Chicago and completed her Ph.D. at Columbia University in 1903. Her main interest was petrology, but Columbia needed teachers for graduate courses in glacial geology, so she made that one of her specialties.

In 1903 Ogilvie founded and headed the geology department at Barnard, Columbia's college for women. She was known for being a supportive teacher and an engaging lecturer. Although she rarely published her work, she conducted research in Maine, New York, California, and Mexico.

In addition to teaching, Dr. Ogilvie had a farm in Bedford, New York, where she raised cattle and other livestock. During World War I, many women went there to learn about agriculture as part of a group called the Women's Land Army. Several of them stayed on to operate a larger farm Ogilvie bought later. She retired from Barnard in 1941 but continued farming. Her hobby was knitting blankets with geologic designs.

Jennie R. Patrick (1949–)
Chemical engineer

JENNIE PATRICK'S PARENTS HAD LITTLE EDUCATION, so they made sure that their children had better opportunities. At her segregated elementary school in Alabama, Jennie had talented and supportive African American teachers. Her years at an integrated high school were marked by the racism of many of the white students and staff. Even in this difficult situation, Patrick graduated with honors.

Patrick began college at Tuskegee Institute but transferred to the University of California at Berkeley. She attended the Massachusetts Institute of Technology and in 1979 became the first African American woman in the country to earn a doctorate in chemical engineering. Patrick worked as a researcher for Dow Chemical, General Electric, and other companies.

In 1993 she returned to Tuskegee to join the chemical engineering faculty. It has always been important to her to guide and inspire African American students interested in the sciences. More recently she has spoken out on health and safety in the workplace. As a result of her years in the research laboratory, Patrick has developed serious allergies to a wide range of common chemical substances. The experience inspired her to encourage others to be vigilant about their working environment and not rely on employers to keep them safe.

Cecilia Payne-Gaposchkin (1900–1979)
Astronomer

ENGLISHWOMAN CECILIA PAYNE STUDIED SCIENCE at Cambridge University but left her home country to pursue graduate studies at Radcliffe College in Massachusetts. In 1925 she became the first person to graduate from Radcliffe with a Ph.D. in astronomy.

After analyzing many stars' spectra for her doctoral dissertation, Payne concluded that hydrogen and helium were more abundant on the sun and other stars than on Earth. However, this contradicted the popular theories of the day. At her supervisor's urging, Payne questioned the accuracy of her findings in her paper. It was nevertheless considered a brilliant work, and several years later her observations were confirmed.

After 1925 Payne worked at the Harvard College Observatory, although she encountered frequent

> "Young people, especially young women, often ask me for advice. Here it is . . . Do not undertake a scientific career in quest of fame or money. There are easier and better ways to reach them. Undertake it only if nothing else will satisfy you; for nothing else is probably what you will receive. Your reward will be the widening of the horizon as you climb. And if you achieve that reward you will ask no other."
>
> CECILIA PAYNE-GAPOSCHKIN
> *An Autobiography and Other Recollections*, 1984

discrimination there. Until 1938 she was considered a technical assistant, not an astronomer. She taught classes, but they weren't listed in the course catalog until 1945. Still, she didn't allow anything to halt her career, even raising the three children she had with her husband, astronomer Sergei Gaposchkin. When Donald Menzel became director of the observatory in 1956, he made her chair of the astronomy department. She retired in 1966 but continued researching until her death.

Marguerite Perey (1909–1975)
Physicist

MARGUERITE PEREY WAS BORN IN VILLENOBLE, France. From childhood she wanted to become a doctor. After her father died, though, the family became very poor. A medical education was too expensive, but she was able to study physics instead.

In 1929 Marguerite began working as a junior laboratory assistant to Marie Curie at the Radium Institute in Paris. She planned to spend just three months there but soon changed her mind. Curie, impressed with Perey's talent and dedication, became a mentor to the young scientist. They worked together until Marie's death. Afterward Perey continued the laboratory's research on radioactive materials.

Perey's most famous discovery came in 1939, while she was studying the radioactive decay of the element actinium. As she tried to interpret the results, she realized another, unfamiliar, element was being formed. Perey decided to call it francium, in honor of France.

In 1940 Perey began working for the National Center for Scientific Research. She became a professor of nuclear physics at the University of Strasbourg in 1949 and was later made director of the Strasbourg Nuclear Research Center. In 1962 she became the first woman ever inducted into the French Academy of Sciences. By that time she was undergoing treatment for cancer, caused by her work with radiation. After 15 years she lost her battle with the disease.

Rózsa Péter (1905–1977)
Mathematician, logician

RÓZSA PÉTER BEGAN BY STUDYING CHEMISTRY AT the Eötvös Loránd University in her hometown of Budapest, Hungary, but she was soon attracted to mathematics. She graduated in 1927 and, after working as a tutor, began graduate studies. A paper on mathematical logic, which she presented at the 1932 International Mathematics Conference in Zurich, brought her recognition in the field. In 1937, two years after receiving her Ph.D., Rózsa joined the editorial board of the Journal of Symbolic Logic.

During World War II, many intellectuals were prevented from teaching by the Fascist Hungarian government. Péter spent those years writing about mathematics. She was one of the developers of a kind of reasoning known as recursive function theory, and she helped establish logic as an accepted field of mathematics. Péter was a professor at the teachers' college

> **"I am inclined to believe that one of the origins of mathematics is man's playful nature, and for this reason mathematics is not only a Science, but to at least the same extent also an Art."**
>
> RÓZSA PÉTER
> *Playing with Infinity*

in Budapest from 1945 until it closed in 1955. She spent the next 20 years at Eötvös Loránd University.

A gifted, inspiring teacher whose students called her Aunt Rózsa, Péter worked to bridge the gap between science and the humanities. Her book *Playing with Infinity* (1943) explained mathematics for the layperson. It was translated into 14 languages. She wrote and translated poetry and gave lectures with such titles as "Mathematics Is Beautiful."

Elena Popescu (1887–1944)
Inventor

ONE DAY WHILE THE 14-YEAR-OLD ROMANIAN schoolgirl Elena Popescu was on vacation, she met an elderly woman who was having difficulty threading a needle. Elena, determined to make the task easier, experimented with several materials and designs and finally made a needle-threading device out of steel wire. All the women in the neighborhood wanted one. With help from her younger brother, she produced about 30 needle threaders. When her school vacation ended, so did her career as an inventor. Her accomplishment might have been forgotten—like the innovations of so many women—if her son had not passed on the story, learned from family accounts and by reading her extensive journals, many of which were lost during World War II.

Elena always rebelled against Romanian society's notion of womanhood. She was able to avoid an arranged marriage and wed the man she loved, Nicolas Copaciu. While he was away fighting in World War I, she took over his duties as leader of an ammunition train. During a shopping excursion to Bucharest, Elena saw a needle threader much like the one she had invented 20 years earlier. The sign next to it said, "Recently invented in the USA."

Edith H. Quimby (1891–1982)
Medical physicist

EDITH HINKLEY WAS BORN IN ILLINOIS, BUT HER family moved frequently while she was growing up. She earned her master's degree in physics from the University of California at Berkeley. In 1919

she and her new husband, Shirley L. Quimby, moved to New York. She began researching the medical uses of radiation when she was hired by Dr. Gioacchino Failla, chief physicist at the New York City Memorial Hospital for Cancer and Allied Diseases. In 1942 she and Failla founded the Radiological Research Laboratory at Columbia University's medical school. Their exceptional partnership lasted 40 years.

One of Quimby's important achievements was developing an exact method for measuring the doses of radiation given to cancer patients. This made treatment more effective and caused fewer harmful side effects. Concerned for the safety of workers who handled radioactive material, she instituted a program in which everyone wore badges made of X-ray film that could be used to estimate a person's degree of exposure.

Quimby was a respected professor at Columbia and a prolific writer. She also participated in research on the atomic bomb and worked for the Atomic Energy Commission. Among her professional honors are the 1957 American Cancer Society Medal. She officially retired in 1960 but remained active into her 80s.

Marie Gertrude Rand (1886–1970)
Lighting engineer, experimental psychologist

GERTRUDE RAND CREATED MORE EFFECTIVE industrial lighting and modern vision-assessment tools. Her technical expertise was enhanced by her training in psychology and her focus on color perception. A native of Brooklyn, New York, she attended college at Columbia University and then earned her master's and doctoral degrees in psychology from Bryn Mawr. She married a colleague, Clarence Ferree, in 1918.

An ideal research team, the couple produced such innovations as the "the Ferree-Rand" perimeter, which helped diagnose vision problems. They patented many of their devices and often served as consultants to industries. Their most famous project was designing the lighting for the Holland Tunnel, which links New York City and New Jersey. In addition to their research, both taught at Johns Hopkins University in Baltimore.

After Ferree's death in 1943, Rand accepted a post at Columbia University. There she helped develop the Hardy-Rand-Rittler plates for the assessment of color vision. The plates aided doctors in determining the type and severity of a patient's color blindness. In 1952 Rand became the first woman fellow of the Illuminating Engineering Society. Seven years later she was the first woman to win the Edgar D. Tillyer Medal of the Optical Society of America.

Mina Spiegel Rees (1902–1997)
Mathematician

MINA REES GREW UP IN NEW YORK CITY AND attended Hunter College, where she was asked to teach a trigonometry course after her freshman year. Following her graduation in 1923, she continued teaching, while also taking classes at Columbia University. However, she soon discovered that Columbia didn't support women doctoral candidates in mathematics. In 1931, having earned a Ph.D. from the University of Chicago, she resumed her career at Hunter.

During World War II, Rees worked for the Office of Scientific Research and Development evaluating math problems posed by the military and assigning the appropriate experts to solve them. Her efforts earned her the United States President's Certificate of Merit and the British King's Medal for Service in the Cause of Freedom in 1948. Rees went on to work for the Office of Naval Research and become an influential member of several national committees.

Rees returned to Hunter College as a professor and dean of the faculty in 1953. She became dean of graduate students at the newly formed City University of New York in 1961 and

president of that institution's Graduate School and University Center eight years later. Her many accomplishments include becoming the first woman president of the American Association for the Advancement of Science.

Maria Reiche (1903–1998)
Mathematician, archaeologist

WHEN MARIA REICHE DIED, AUTHORITIES IN the town of Nazca, Peru, declared a day of mourning. For over 50 years, Reiche had studied and protected their archaeological treasure, the Nazca Lines. There are 13,000 lines, or patterns, etched into the earth by the Nazca people from 370 B.C.E. to 450 C.E. They include spirals, straight lines, and animals—and they are so large that they must be viewed from an airplane for the shapes to be recognizable.

Marie Reiche with an assistant

Born in Dresden, Germany, Reiche had majored in mathematics in college and had come to Peru in 1932 to work as a tutor. She met historian Paul Kosok at the University of San Marcos and studied the lines with him before taking over the project in 1948. Kosok and Reiche discovered that many, if not all, of the figures are related to astronomy, but their true purpose remains a mystery. Reiche also determined the sophisticated geometric methods used by the Nazca artists to produce such gigantic shapes. They are still visible after over 2,000 years because the desert at Nazca is exceptionally dry and windless. There is almost no erosion on the surface of the ground.

Reiche's writings include the book *Secret of the Pampas* (1968). In 1993 her project was declared a Cultural Heritage of Mankind by the United Nations Educational, Scientific, and Cultural Organization (UNESCO).

Doris Livesey Reynolds (1899–1985)
Geologist

In 1920 Doris Livesey Reynolds graduated with first-class honors from Bedford College at the University of London. She taught at colleges in England and Ireland while pursuing graduate studies in geology and received her doctorate from the University of London in 1937. She was an honorary research fellow at the University of Edinburgh from 1943 to 1962.

Most of Reynolds's research focused on granitization, the process by which various kinds of rocks are converted into granite. One of her most significant contributions was her discovery of the role of fluidization in rock formation. Fluidization, causing solid particles to act like a fluid by suspending them in liquid or gas, is a useful industrial technique. Reynolds found that a similar process occurs at subvolcanic levels in the earth, where flowing gases can carry in some materials and remove others, changing the chemical composition of the surrounding rock. Her work earned her the 1960 Lyell Medal from the Geological Society of London.

In 1962 Dr. Reynolds accepted a position at Bedford College. In addition to numerous articles, she published a textbook, *Elements of Physical Geology*, in 1969. After her husband, geologist Arthur Holmes, died, she revised his *Holmes' Principles of Physical Geology* for its third edition.

Ida Rhodes (1900–1986)
Mathematician, computer scientist

Ida Rhodes was born Hadassah Itzkowitz in a Jewish village in the Ukraine. Her name was changed after her family moved to the United States in 1913. A gifted mathematician, Ida received a scholarship to Cornell University in New York. In addition to taking classes, she also worked as a nurse's aide at Ithaca City Hospital. In 1923 she received both her bachelor's and master's degrees in mathematics.

After holding various jobs, Rhodes began her long career with the National Bureau of Standards (NBS) in 1940. Her first assignment was with the Math Tables Project, calculating tables and solving problems for government and industry. Many of the workers on the project were high school graduates or physically handicapped people who needed work during the Great Depression. Rhodes helped to train, encourage, and inspire them.

In 1947 Rhodes moved to Washington, D.C., to work on the UNIVAC I, one of the first digital computers. She continued her pioneering efforts in computer science at the NBS until she retired in 1964. Among other accomplishments, she designed the original computer program for the Social Security Administration. Rhodes was also a generous supporter of Jewish causes.

Ellen Swallow Richards (1842–1911)
Chemist, ecologist, home economist

In 1875 Ellen Swallow completed the doctoral program in chemistry at the Massachusetts Institute of Technology, but she never received the Ph.D. The administrators didn't want to award the first doctorate in chemistry to a woman. Still, they were delighted to have her teach there. She spent over 25 years on the faculty.

In 1876, the year she married mining engineering professor Robert Richards, Ellen began using her scientific skills to study the environment. A pioneer in ecology, she analyzed water and sewer samples for the Massachusetts Board of Health and worked in MIT's sanitation chemistry department.

She always tried to help aspiring women scientists. From 1876 until 1883, Richards operated the Woman's Laboratory, a scientific training facility at MIT. She conducted studies to show that, contrary to popular belief, academic women didn't experience poorer health than other women. She also helped create the field of home economics. Richards felt that a scientific education would help mothers maintain healthy families. She knew this idea would please

traditionalists who thought women's place was in the home. At the same time, it allowed women to obtain a better education.

Richards turned her Boston house into the Center for Right Living, a laboratory where she tested everything from plumbing to prepared foods. She gave lectures, devised school curricula, and published such books as *The Chemistry of Cooking and Cleaning* (1882). She served as president of the American Home Economics Association from 1908 until she retired in 1910.

Theodate Pope Riddle (1868–1946)
Architect

THEODATE POPE WAS INDEPENDENT EVEN AS A child. She thrived at Miss Porter's School for Girls in Connecticut, where her ambitions were nurtured. Because architectural training was difficult for women to obtain, she created her own apprenticeship: She designed a house for her parents, hired the famous firm of McKim, Mead, and White to prepare the working drawings, and paid close attention to every phase of the process. The house is now the Hill-Stead Museum in Farmington.

Pope was best known for the schools she built in Connecticut. In 1910 she designed and helped establish the Westover School for Girls in Middlebury. Her most famous project was the Avon Old Farms boys school, designed in the style of an antique English

village. The school provided an agricultural education and encouraged self-government among students.

Among other projects, Pope supervised the construction of the Theodore Roosevelt Memorial, a reconstruction of his birthplace on its original site in New York City. A member of the social elite, she was active in many organizations, including the Colonial Dames of America. She was elected to the American Institute of Architects in 1918. Pope married a diplomat, John Riddle, at the age of 49 but continued to use her own name professionally.

Sally Ride (1951–)
Physicist, astronaut

CALIFORNIAN SALLY RIDE'S TALENTS AS A TENNIS player could have led to a professional sports career—she was once ranked 18th nationally at the junior level. Instead, she was inspired to study science by her high school teacher Dr. Elizabeth Mommaerts. She majored in English and physics at Stanford University and entered the graduate program in physics there. In 1978, as she was finishing her Ph.D., she applied to NASA's astronaut training program and was one of 35 people accepted.

Ride had focused on physics, astronomy, and astrophysics at Stanford. NASA's program involved further studies in mathematics, meteorology, and navigation; she also had to earn her pilot's license. On June 18, 1983, Ride became the youngest person and the first American woman in space. She spent six days aboard the space shuttle *Challenger*, operating the shuttle's robot arm and conducting experiments. She participated in her second *Challenger* flight in October 1984.

That same year the Institute for Public Service honored Ride with its Jefferson Award for her commitment to teaching children about space exploration. She has published several children's books, including

To Space and Back (1986), written with her friend Susan Okie. Since 1989 Ride has been a professor of physics and the director of the California Space Institute at the University of California at San Diego.

Dorothea Klumpke Roberts (1861–1942)
Astronomer

Dorothea Klumpke was born in San Francisco, but her mother took the family to Europe in order to provide an equal education for her sons and daughters. Dorothea earned her undergraduate degree at the University of Paris. In 1886 she became the first woman accepted as a student and a staff member at the Paris Observatory.

Klumpke's work focused on using photographic plates to determine the location of the stars. Between 1891 and 1901, she served as the director of the Bureau of Measurements, a department dedicated to administering the observatory's contribution to the international project to catalog the entire sky. Her superb work led to her election as the first woman officer of the Paris Academy of Sciences in 1893. That same year she received the first doctorate in mathematics granted to a woman by the University of Paris.

In 1901 Dorothea married Welsh astronomer Isaac Roberts. They worked together at his private observatory

in Sussex, England, until his death in 1904. In 1934 President Albert Lebrun of France awarded Dorothea the cross of the Legion of Honor. After retiring, she returned to San Francisco with her sister, and their home became a meeting place for scientists and artists. Her donations to various astronomical societies provided support for the education of young astronomers.

Mabel MacFerran Rockwell (1902–1981)
Electrical engineer

In 1925 Mabel Rockwell graduated first in her class with a teaching and science degree from the Massachusetts Institute of Technology. She continued her studies at Stanford University, earning a degree in electrical engineering the following year. Hired by the Southern California Edison Company, Rockwell helped determine the location of malfunctions in multiple power lines. Later, as an assistant engineer at the Metropolitan Water District of Southern California, she worked on the Colorado River Aqueduct Power System. She was also the only woman engineer involved in the electrical installations for Hoover Dam.

In 1940 Rockwell was hired by Lockheed Aircraft Corporation, where she worked to streamline and improve the methods used to build military aircraft. Among her contributions were several innovations in welding techniques.

Rockwell went on to contribute to missile development technology, working for the Westinghouse Electric Company's defense division and for Convair (Consolidated-Vultee Aircraft Corporation). She also served as an editor in the engineering department at Stanford University. Her treatment of scholarly papers was so thorough that it became known as "Mabelizing." In 1958 she was named Woman Engineer of the Year by President Dwight Eisenhower and received the Society of Women Engineers Achievement Award.

Emily Warren Roebling (1843–1903)
Self-taught engineer

EMILY WARREN GREW UP IN A PROMINENT FAMILY IN Cold Spring, New York. She must have anticipated a rather ordinary life as a housewife when she married Washington Roebling in 1865. Both Washington and his father, John Roebling, were engineers. John was directing the construction of what was then the world's longest suspension bridge, which would connect New York City and Brooklyn (then two separate cities). However, he died in 1869 after being injured on the site. Washington took his place but was soon rendered partially blind, paralyzed, and almost mute by the "bends." This painful condition results from returning too quickly to the surface after spending time underwater, where the atmospheric pressure is very high. The rapid decrease in air pressure causes bubbles to form in the tissues of the body.

Washington taught Emily the basics of engineering, including mathematics, stress analysis, and cable construction. For 11 years she directed the monumental project herself, communicating with the workers and consulting with her husband as necessary. In 1882 she became the first woman to address the American Society of Civil Engineers when she urged them not to replace Washington as official director of the project.

Although Emily was the first person to cross the Brooklyn Bridge and her name appears on a plaque there, she received no credit in the official construction documents. She remained active in the community, most notably in relief efforts during the Spanish American War.

Marguerite Hessein de la Sablière (1640–1693)
Scientific writer, salon hostess

DURING THE 1600s THERE WERE FEW AVENUES OF study available to women in France and England, so they developed their own, inviting intellectuals to salons so they could discuss science, literature, and art. Madame de la Sablière was one such woman.

Marguerite Hessein married Antoine de Rambouillet, sieur de la Sablière in 1654. They had three children but eventually separated. She went on to establish one of the most popular salons in Paris. Marguerite studied astronomy, mathematics, and physics with members of the French Academy of Sciences, owned a telescope, and wrote at least one scientific paper. She became a patron of the fable writer Jean La Fontaine. Her intelligence and unassuming attitude won her the respect of many, and she was awarded an annual pension by the king. However, there were people who resented "scientific ladies." In Nicolas Boileau-Despréaux's *Satire contres les femmes* (1694, A satire against women), Madame de la Sablière is portrayed with failing eyesight and a ruined complexion due to her studies in astronomy.

Marguerite de la Sablière turned to the study of religion and converted to Catholicism in the 1680s. She spent her later years living a cloistered life and tending to patients at a Paris hospital.

Saruhashi Katsuko (1920–)
Marine geochemist

WHEN SARUHASHI KATSUKO WAS IN COLLEGE at Toho University in Japan, scientific equipment was scarce. Fortunately Miyake Yasuo, a government meteorologist, invited her to use his laboratory. After graduating in 1943, Saruhashi accepted a job at Miyake's Geochemical Laboratory and became one of the first people to study carbon dioxide levels in the ocean. Many scientists now believe the increasing concentration of carbon dioxide on Earth contributes to global warming. Saruhashi used this research for her graduate work and in 1957 became the first woman to earn a doctorate in chemistry from Tokyo University.

Saruhashi studied other environmental problems, too. In 1954 the United States tested a hydrogen bomb on Bikini Island in the Pacific Ocean. After crew members from a Japanese fishing boat became ill from the fallout, Saruhashi began monitoring radiation levels in rainwater and seawater and measuring how far the contamination had spread. In the 1970s she turned her attention to acid rain.

Improving the status of women scientists in Japan is a longstanding concern for Dr. Saruhashi. She established the Society of Japanese Women Scientists in 1958 and in 1980 founded both the Association for the Bright Future of Women Scientists and the Saruhashi Prize for women in science. She has received considerable recognition herself, including the 1993 Tanaka Prize from the Society of Sea Water Science.

Salyut 7 space station, where she spent eight days conducting experiments. In July 1984 she became the first woman to walk in space. She is married to fellow engineer Viktor Khatovsky, and they have one son.

Svetlana Savitskaya (1948–)
Aeronautical engineer, cosmonaut

COSMONAUT SVETLANA SAVITSKAYA WAS FIRST inspired to travel in space by her father, an officer in the Soviet air force and head of air defense for the country. She learned to pilot and parachute as a teenager. She attended an aerotechnical school as a teenager and went to college at the Moscow Aviation Institute. In 1972 she received a degree in aeronautical engineering.

Savitskaya went on to work as a design engineer for Yakovlev Aircraft. She was also a talented and daring pilot. During her test flights, she established several speed records, and she won many competitions. In 1970 she became the first woman to earn first place in all-around flying at the World Aerobatics Championships in Great Britain.

In 1980 Savitskaya joined the Soviet Cosmonaut program. Two years later she became the second woman ever to travel into space (the first was Valentina Tereshkova, also a Soviet cosmonaut). Savitskaya flew aboard the *Soyuz T-7* spacecraft to the

Charlotte Angas Scott (1858–1931)
Mathematician

IN 1880 CHARLOTTE SCOTT, AN UNOFFICIAL student at Girton College, received the eighth-highest score on the mathematics honors examination given by Cambridge University. This accomplishment ought to have earned her the title "eighth wrangler" (a term taken from ancient Greek scholarly debates, in which the Greek word for *disputant* was translated into English as *wrangler*). Instead the honor was given to an official male student. Scott's peers knew the truth, however. At the point when her name should have been announced, they cheered and chanted "Scott of Girton! Scott of Girton!"

After earning her doctorate from the University of London in 1885, the British mathematician was invited to be one of the first six faculty members at Bryn Mawr College in Pennsylvania. She created an outstanding math department there, and her clear, exciting lectures inspired students at both the undergraduate and graduate levels.

Scott was a founder of the American Mathematical Society and in 1904 became the organization's first woman vice-president. In addition to publishing over 30 papers and editing the *American Journal of Mathematics*, she wrote a textbook, *An Introductory*

Account of Certain Modern Ideas in Plane Analytical Geometry (1894), that was used for many years.

A beloved professor who was known for her spectacular flower garden as well as her gift for teaching, Charlotte Scott was honored by Bryn Mawr at a special ceremony in 1922. She retired three years later and spent her last years in England.

Patsy Sherman (1930–)
Chemist, inventor

PATSY SHERMAN WAS BORN IN MINNEAPOLIS, Minnesota, and attended Gustavus Adolphus College in the town of St. Peter. She began working for the Minnesota Mining & Manufacturing Company—also known as 3M—in 1952, shortly after her graduation. One of the company's goals was to create new products from polymers that contain the element fluorine. Her specific assignment was to develop a new rubber compound that would not deteriorate when exposed to jet fuel.

One day a laboratory assistant dropped a beaker of a latex compound on the floor, and it splashed on her sneakers. Sherman tried without success to help the assistant wash it off. After noticing that the compound also repelled all the solutions they were using on it, Sherman realized they might have a new product. Three years later, she and chemist Sam Smith received a patent for Scotchgard, which is now used to coat carpets, upholstery, and other fabrics, making them stainproof.

Sherman retired from 3M in 1992, having spent four decades there. She often gives speeches on her experiences and encourages young people who are interested in the sciences and invention.

Donna Shirley (1941–)
Aeronautical engineer

AS A TEN-YEAR-OLD IN SMALL-TOWN WYNNEWOOD, Oklahoma, Donna Shirley decided she wanted to be an aeronautical engineer. Before she finished high school, she could fly a plane. An adviser discouraged her from majoring in engineering at the University of Oklahoma. But after earning a degree in writing, she went back for a bachelor of science degree and graduated in 1965.

Donna Shirley with the **Sojourner** *rover*

In 1966 Shirley moved to Pasadena, California, to work at NASA's Jet Propulsion Laboratory (JPL). She also studied for her master's degree at the University of Southern California. She worked her way up at JPL, sometimes struggling to prove herself to her male colleagues, especially after she married and had a daughter. In the late 1980s, she was asked to lead a team to design a vehicle for exploring Mars.

The first rover they planned would have weighed one ton (907 kg) and cost ten billion dollars. Shirley realized this was too expensive. She was convinced that a much smaller rover would work just as well. Her team finally devised a six-wheeled rover that weighed just 25 pounds (11 kg). It was named after the African American abolitionist Sojourner Truth. After traveling for seven months aboard the spacecraft *Pathfinder*, the rover arrived on Mars on July 4, 1997. Exceeding even its triumphant creators' expectations, *Sojourner* transmitted pictures and other data back to Earth for 12 weeks. Shirley published a memoir, *Managing Martians*, in 1998.

Hannah Slater (1776?–1812)
Inventor

HANNAH WILKINSON GREW UP IN A QUAKER family in Pawtucket, Rhode Island. She was 17 years old when she married Samuel Slater. Samuel was building mills to manufacture cotton yarn for weaving and knitting. He had learned about the machinery in his home country, England, and had only recently come to America, where his skills were desperately needed in the fledgling textile manufacturing industry. He eventually became famous as one of New England's first industrial capitalists. Hannah did not become well known, although her invention played a significant role in his success.

During the 1700s most people used linen thread for sewing. One day, while Hannah was spinning cotton, she wondered if it would make good sewing thread. She experimented with the cotton by twisting together double strands. Eventually she created a thread that was stronger and easier to use than linen. The invention was patented, and in 1798 Samuel Slater & Company began producing and marketing the thread. Hannah died at age 37, after the birth of her sixth child.

Mary Fairfax Somerville (1780–1872)
Mathematician, science writer

EXCEPT FOR AN UNHAPPY YEAR AT A GIRLS' boarding school, the Scottish mathematician Mary Somerville had little formal education. When she was 15 years old, she became fascinated with a page of equations that she found in a magazine. Upon learning that it was algebra, she obtained math books from her brother's tutor and read them on her own.

Mary's studies were interrupted during her three-year marriage to Samuel Greig, but she resumed them after his death in 1807. Her second husband,

William Somerville, whom she married in 1812, fully encouraged her interests. They moved from the Scottish town of Burntisland to London, where they socialized with many scientists and intellectuals.

Somerville's first three published papers discussed experiments about the sun, and she was commissioned to translate *Mécanique céleste*, written by Pierre-Simon Laplace. Her *Mechanism of the Heavens*, published in 1831, included her commentary alongside the translation. It would be used as a textbook for the next century. That year a bust of Mary Somerville was placed on display at London's Royal Society.

Somerville hesitated to publish her third book, *Physical Geography* (1848), because the famed scientist Alexander von Humboldt had also written on the topic. She need not have worried. Humboldt admired her work and urged her to proceed with its publication. After her death at age 92, Somerville College at Oxford University was named for her.

Mary Spaeth (1940–)
Physicist, inventor

TEXAS NATIVE MARY SPAETH KNEW HOW TO USE woodworking tools by the time she was three years old. At eight she figured out a way to make reclosable cereal boxes—a method identical to the one used today (which cereal companies introduced years later). She became interested in physics during the seventh grade and went on to earn a master's degree at Michigan's Wayne State University in 1962. That same year she accepted a position at Hughes Aircraft Company.

During a break between research projects there, Spaeth started investigating ways to create a new type of laser. At the time the color of a laser beam had to be chosen when the apparatus was built; it couldn't be changed later. It took Spaeth just two weeks to develop a prototype for a "tunable dye laser," which emitted different colors as needed. Her useful innovation meant that a single laser could perform multiple tasks.

Spaeth also invented the resonant reflector, the laser technology that made the bar-code scanners used in grocery stores possible. The research was commissioned by the army but is used in many everyday situations. Spaeth left the Hughes Aircraft Company in 1974. She has continued her research at Lawrence Livermore National Laboratory in California.

Rebecca Hall Sparling (1910–1996)
Mechanical engineer

REBECCA SPARLING WAS THE TENTH CHILD BORN to well-educated parents in Memphis, Tennessee. She attended both undergraduate and graduate school at Vanderbilt University and earned her master's degree in physical chemistry in 1931. Afterward she worked as a consultant for several companies. Her expertise was in metallurgy, and in 1944 she published *American Malleable Iron*, which became a widely used textbook.

From 1944 to 1951, Sparling worked at Northrop Aircraft as chief materials engineer. She was then hired as a design specialist at General Dynamics in California, where she remained until her retirement in 1968. Her job was to choose and test materials for building aircraft. She developed time-saving methods for subjecting materials to high temperatures and ways of evaluating their performance under stressful conditions without destroying them. Much of her work was classified information, because it focused on missile and aerospace technology.

Sparling was active in protecting the environment. She helped found the Desert Environment Conservation Association and was a member of the San Bernardino County Air Pollution Board. She also made a point of encouraging women students to pursue careers in engineering. In 1978 Sparling was honored with the Outstanding Engineering Merit Award from the Institute for the Advancement of Engineering.

Jill Cornell Tarter (1944–)
Astronomer

DR. JILL TARTER HAS DEVOTED HER CAREER TO THE search for extraterrestrial life. It is a controversial mission to some people, but many scientists agree that it's worth pursuing. Within our own galaxy alone, there are billions of stars, and it is not unreasonable to think that at least one planet orbiting one of those stars might support a technologically advanced civilization.

Tarter went to college at Cornell University and then earned a doctorate in astrophysics from the University of California at Berkeley. She was working at NASA's Ames Research Center when she met

Waiting for a Message

Jill Tarter and her colleagues at SETI have dedicated themselves to listening for evidence of extraterrestrial life. Why don't they send out messages, too? Partly because the inhabitants of Earth are constantly sending messages. Our television and radio signals travel far into space, where other life forms could intercept them. Besides, even if SETI sent a message to the closest solar system they have targeted and the inhabitants replied immediately, SETI wouldn't receive a response for eight years— because that system is four light-years away. As Tarter explains, "Listening could be more of an instant-gratification scheme."

astronomer Frank Drake, who had begun to search for signs of life from outer space. In 1984 she helped to found the SETI (Search for Extraterrestrial Intelligence) program at Ames.

In 1993 NASA withdrew its funding, but private donors helped SETI survive. As director of Project Phoenix, Tarter manages studies in Puerto Rico, West Virginia, and New Mexico. She and her team use huge radio telescopes pointed at strategic locations in the sky to gather electromagnetic signals from space. So far, they haven't found anything.

However, this search is bound to take time. Even the nearest solar system is four light-years away. Tarter, a mother of three, does not worry that her research might not show any results during her lifetime. She considers scientists' willingness to undertake such a long-term project a "maturing phase in our civilization."

Maria Telkes (1900–1995)
Solar engineer, chemist

MARIA TELKES WAS A HIGH SCHOOL STUDENT when she began reading about solar energy in books written in English, French, German, and her native Hungarian. She attended the University of Budapest and ultimately earned her Ph.D. in physical

chemistry. In 1925, during a visit to the United States, she was hired by the Cleveland Clinic Foundation to study energy changes in cells. In 1937 she became an American citizen.

In 1939 Telkes began working on the Solar Energy Conversion Project at the Massachusetts Institute of Technology. She developed a new solar heating system, in which the sun's energy was absorbed by sodium sulfate solution. This chemical would crystallize and then release the energy as heat. In 1948 Telkes and architect Eleanor Raymond designed a house that utilized this system.

Dr. Telkes went on to improve the process of removing salt from seawater. While working for the Office of Scientific Research and Development, she designed a sun-powered distillation system to provide drinking water on lifeboats and then adapted it for larger-scale use in the Virgin Islands. She also developed solar-powered ovens. In 1977, the year before her retirement, Telkes was honored for her contributions to solar energy engineering by the National Academy of Science's Building Research Advisory Board.

Marie Tharp (1920–)
Geologist, oceanographic cartographer

A S A GIRL MARIE THARP ATTENDED 24 DIFFERENT schools because her family moved so often to accommodate her father's job as a government surveyor. She earned a master's degree in geology at the University of Michigan in 1944. After working for an oil company in Oklahoma, she was hired by geologist Maurice Ewing at Columbia University, where she met her longtime collaborator, Bruce Heezen.

Most geologists at the time did not accept the theory of continental drift, which holds that the land on Earth was originally a solid mass that began breaking apart over 200 million years ago and slowly formed the six continents. Tharp and Heezen were using sonar (sound echoes) to map the ocean floor. As they plotted the terrain of the Mid-Atlantic Ridge,

an undersea mountain chain that runs north to south between Africa and the Americas, they discovered geological formations that strongly supported the continental drift idea. Their work was instrumental in persuading the scientific community to change their minds about the theory.

In 1998 Tharp was one of four cartographers honored at the centennial of the Library of Congress's geography and map division. Reminiscing about Heezen, who died in 1977, she has written that she always wanted to include mermaids and shipwrecks on the areas of the map that were incomplete, but that he wouldn't let her. Tharp and Heezen's map, *The World Ocean Floor Panorama* (1977), is still widely used.

Theano (6th–5th century B.C.E.)
Mathematician, philosopher, physician

T HEANO WAS A FOLLOWER OF PYTHAGORAS, AN ancient Greek philosopher who founded a scholarly community in what is now Crotone, Italy. The Pythagorean school was based on the study of politics, religion, philosophy, and mathematics.

Few details of Theano's role in the history of mathematics and science are known, not only because she lived centuries ago, but also because the community was secretive and members' ideas were often credited to Pythagoras. Theano was certainly a skilled mathematician and healer. She was a student and then a teacher at Pythagoras's school. She is thought to have been his wife as well.

It is believed that Pythagoras was killed around 500 B.C.E. by rebels who resented his power in the local government. The community did leave the area around that time. Some sources say that Theano then became their leader and helped to spread their teachings through Greece and Egypt.

Florence Van Straten (1913–)
Meteorologist

CONNECTICUT-BORN FLORENCE VAN STRATEN wanted to be a writer, but her father convinced her to study science, as well as English, at New York University. She was so good at chemistry that during her senior year she substituted for the professor teaching the freshman chemistry course. She earned her Ph.D. in chemistry in 1939.

During World War II, Van Straten joined the naval program, Women Accepted for Voluntary Service (WAVES). She studied meteorology and began reporting weather conditions to ships in the Pacific Ocean. She also became interested in the possibility of using science to control the weather. One of her theories was that the evaporation rate within a cloud determined whether or not rain would occur.

After the war Van Straten became director of the Technical Requirements Branch of the U.S. Navy and continued her research on weather modification. In 1956 the navy recognized her contributions with the Meritorious Civilian Service Award. Two years later she successfully used carbon particles to create and dissipate clouds. After her retirement in 1962, Van Straten continued to work as a consultant. She also returned to her dream of being a writer, publishing works for general audiences.

Anna Johnson Pell Wheeler (1883–1966)
Mathematician

THE DAUGHTER OF SWEDISH IMMIGRANTS, ANNA Johnson grew up in Iowa and began her studies at the University of South Dakota in 1899. There Professor Alexander Pell encouraged her interest in mathematics. Pell, a Russian immigrant, had been a double agent in his home country. The dashing teacher and his talented student soon fell in love.

After earning master's degrees at both the University of Iowa and Radcliffe College, Anna went to Göttingen University in Germany in 1906. While she was abroad, she married Pell and wrote her doctoral dissertation. However, she and her adviser, David Hilbert, argued about the content, so she completed her Ph.D. at the University of Chicago.

As a woman she had difficulty finding a teaching job until she was hired by Mount Holyoke College in 1911. Seven years later she moved to Bryn Mawr College, where she eventually became head of the mathematics department. She was widowed in 1921 and later married Arthur Wheeler, a classics professor.

Anna Wheeler was listed as one of the top mathematicians in the 1921 edition of *American Men of Science* (which did include a few women, despite its title). In 1927 she became the first woman to deliver the Colloquium Lecture to the American Mathematical Society—a prestigious honor. When Emmy Noether, a Jewish mathematician, was forced to flee Nazi Germany, Wheeler gave her a post at Bryn Mawr; the two became good friends.

Mary Watson Whitney (1847–1921)
Astronomer

As a high school student in Waltham, Massachusetts, Mary Whitney eagerly awaited the opening of Vassar College and was among the first students to enroll at the new school in 1865. She was an excellent student in all fields, but astronomer Maria Mitchell soon became her favorite teacher. After graduation Whitney continued her astronomy studies. She attended two courses at Harvard University, even though women were not yet accepted there (she had to wait outside the gates for her professor, Benjamin Peirce, to accompany her to class). In 1872 she earned her master's degree at Vassar and then spent three years studying in Switzerland. Despite her impressive credentials, however, she was unable to find a job at an American university and taught high school for several years.

In 1881 Maria Mitchell hired her as an assistant, and in 1888 Whitney inherited Mitchell's positions as a professor and the director of the Vassar Observatory. She was an effective teacher, who cultivated contacts so that her students could work in observatories all over the United States. She emphasized the study of photographic plates, which would become an essential tool for 19th-century astronomers. Whitney strongly supported the education of women. It is reported that soon before her death she said, "I hope when I get to Heaven I shall not find women playing second fiddle."

Sheila Widnall (1938–)
Aeronautical engineer

As soon as Sheila Evans won the science fair at her high school in Tacoma, Washington, she knew what she wanted to do when she grew up. With enthusiastic encouragement from her parents,

she entered the Massachusetts Institute of Technology in 1956. There were about 900 students in her class—20 of them were women.

Sheila flourished at MIT, choosing aerodynamics as her major. During her senior year, she married fellow student William Widnall and eventually had two children. After completing her Ph.D. in aerodynamics, also at MIT, she was hired as an assistant professor there. She continued her association with the school for the next 19 years, rising to the administrative position of associate provost. Among her accomplishments was designing MIT's anechoic (echo-free) wind tunnel, which is used to study the noise of aircraft during landing and takeoff.

In 1993 Dr. Widnall was appointed Secretary of the Air Force by President Bill Clinton. She was the first woman to occupy that post. She served until 1997 and then returned to teach at MIT. Widnall holds three patents and is a member of several organizations, including the National Academy of Engineering and the American Academy of Arts and Sciences.

Jessie Wright (1900–1970)
Inventor, physician

During the 1930s and 1940s, people who were stricken with polio often suffered paralysis. The chest muscles, which control breathing, were often affected, and patients had to be placed in a machine called an iron lung that forced air in and out of the body. It was during this epidemic that Jessie Wright began practicing medicine.

Wright had been born in England, but her family immigrated to Pittsburgh, Pennsylvania, when she was a girl. She earned her medical degree at the University of Pittsburgh and specialized in physical rehabilitation. In 1945 she created the Respir-Aid, a rocking bed, as an alternative to the iron lung. The bed worked by raising the patient's upper body, which caused air to be drawn into the lungs, then rocking in the other direction to expel the air. It also increased blood circulation and helped some patients begin to breathe on their own again.

Wright invented other physical therapy devices, including several different kinds of splints. She also worked with Dr. Jonas Salk as he perfected his polio vaccine. Her influence was felt outside the United States. In 1957 Argentina honored Wright for her

contributions to controlling polio. Dr. Wright belonged to many organizations, including the American Academy for Cerebral Palsy, for which she served as president in 1962.

Chien-Shiung Wu (1912–1997)
Physicist

WHEN CHIEN-SHIUNG WU WAS INVITED TO attend the National Central University in Nanjing, China, she worried that her scientific background was weak. Her father, ever encouraging, brought her textbooks to study. After earning a mathematics degree, she left for the United States in 1936, little suspecting that World War II and the Communist Revolution would make her an exile. By the time she was able to return in 1973—as an American citizen—her parents had passed away.

Wu earned her Ph.D. from the University of California at Berkeley in 1940, and she married a fellow student, Chi-Liu Yuan, two years later. She held several teaching posts, remaining longest at Columbia University, and participated in the Manhattan Project.

Among Wu's important contributions was her research into the "conservation of parity," a law of physics that says the behavior of molecules and atoms is symmetrical; that is, motion is as likely to occur in one direction as another. Two scientists, Tsung-Dao Lee and Chen Ning Yang, theorized that, although most subatomic particles obeyed the law,

some particles might violate it. Wu designed an experiment that proved them right. Painstakingly observing the decay of radioactive cobalt nuclei, she determined that electrons were usually ejected upward. Her work helped Lee and Yang win the 1957 Nobel Prize for physics.

Wu was overlooked for the Nobel Prize, but she received numerous honors. She was the first woman to win the prestigious Comstock Award from the National Academy of Sciences.

Xie Xide (1921–)
Physicist

WHEN XIE XIDE WAS 16 YEARS OLD, THE Japanese invaded Peking (now Beijing), China, forcing her family to flee. Xie contracted tuberculosis on the way to their new home in Guiyang and spent over three years in the hospital. After earning her physics degree in 1946 from Xiamen University, she went to the United States to attend graduate programs at Smith College and the Massachusetts Institute of Technology. The focus of her research was on the behavior of electrons in gases. In 1951 she earned her Ph.D. in physics.

Dr. Xie traveled to England, where she married biochemist Cao Tianqin, a childhood friend. They moved to Shanghai, and Xie taught at the university there. During the Cultural Revolution of the 1960s, a time when many intellectuals were persecuted, she was held prisoner in her laboratory and then sent to work in a factory.

After Xie was allowed to resume teaching in 1974, she became a leader in science education. In addition to doing physics research, she founded the Modern Physics Institute and was appointed vice-president of Fudan University in Shanghai. In 1982 she became president of the university and was elected to the Central Committee of the Chinese Communist party. She has received international recognition for her work.

Grace Chisholm Young (1868–1944)
Mathematician

AFTER STUDYING MATH AT GIRTON COLLEGE IN England, London-born Grace Chisholm was given permission to attend the University of Göttingen. In 1895 she passed the oral mathematics examination, becoming one of the first women to earn a Ph.D. in Germany. She sent a copy of her dissertation to William Young, her tutor from Girton College. They continued corresponding, and in 1896 they were married.

Grace Young with her son, Frank

The Youngs found that England was not a fertile place for mathematics research, so they settled in Germany, although William often accepted teaching posts abroad. They did much of their work together but usually published under William's name, producing over 200 articles and several books. In 1908 they moved to Switzerland with their six children. Grace completed the coursework for a medical degree there, although she did not go on to practice.

Grace Young made a significant contribution to the field of differential calculus with her work on what came to be known as the Denjoy-Saks-Young theorem. A series of papers she wrote about it between 1914 and 1916 earned her the Gamble Prize from Girton College. At the beginning of World War II, Grace left Switzerland to take two of her grandchildren to England. She was not allowed to return, and William was forbidden to follow her. He died in 1942, thus ending one of the great partnerships in mathematics.

Lai-Sang Young (1952–)
Mathematician

LAI-SANG YOUNG WAS BORN IN HONG KONG, BUT she immigrated to the United States during her youth. She majored in mathematics while at college at the University of Wisconsin. In 1978 she earned her Ph.D. from the University of California at Berkeley. She has taught at several universities in the United States, Great Britain, and Germany. She is currently on the faculty at the University of California at Los Angeles.

Young's specialty is "ergodic" theory, a branch of statistics that focuses on probabilities within systems whose state changes over time. Relatively few mathematicians had addressed this topic until she began her investigations, and she has developed useful new techniques for study. In 1993 the American Mathematical Society awarded Young the Ruth Lyttle Satter Prize for her contributions to mathematics. Four years later she received a Guggenheim Fellowship to help support her work. In addition to her scholarly interests, Dr. Young is a talented table tennis player who once ranked in the top 20 among American women.

TIME LINE

2600 B.C.E.	According to tradition, the wife of Chinese emperor Huang-ti learns how to breed silkworms and devises a way of weaving silken fabric.
6th century B.C.E.	The first books that will later make up the Old Testament are recorded.
5th century B.C.E.	Greek sorceress Aglaonike claims to be able to make the sun and the moon disappear. Her "magic" is more likely astronomy; she has learned to calculate when eclipses will occur.
400–100 B.C.E.	Mayan astronomy is at a high point. An accurate solar calendar is created.
1st century	The books that will later make up the New Testament are written down. Alchemist Maria Prophetissa is active in Alexandria. She is credited with inventing the "water bath," similar to the modern-day double boiler.
415	Inventor and mathematician Hypatia of Alexandria is brutally murdered by Christian monks under the authority of Cyril, the patriarch of Alexandria.

Hypatia of Alexandria

570	Women from China's northern Ch'i province invent matches to start fires for cooking and heating.
1298	The earliest known spinning wheel is invented in Germany.
1434	The printing press is developed by Johann Gutenberg in Mainz, Germany.
1492	Explorer Christopher Columbus lands on an island in the Bahamas, most probably San Salvador, and claims this New World in the name of the Spanish King Ferdinand.
1573	At age 17 Sophia Brahe, the younger sister of Danish astronomer Tycho Brahe, assists her brother with his work and in December observes a lunar eclipse with him.
1633	Italian astronomer and scientist Galileo Galilei goes on trial in Rome to defend the controversial theory introduced by Nicolaus Copernicus, that the Earth revolves around the sun, rather than the reverse. When threatened with torture, he retracts his statement and spends the last nine years of his life confined to his villa outside Florence.
1680s	French astronomer Jeanne Dumée writes *Entretiens sur l'opinion de Copernic touchant la mobilité de la terre* (A treatise on Copernicus's opinion as regards the motion of the Earth) in support of the Copernican and Galilean theories.
1705	French astronomer Edmond Halley concludes that three comet sightings

recorded over the past two centuries have been caused by a single comet. His prediction that the comet will return in 1758–1759 is confirmed by Nicole Lepaute after Halley's death.

1732   Italian physicist Laura Bassi begins delivering lectures on philosophy and science as a professor at the University of Bologna.

1738   Italian philosopher and mathematician Maria Agnesi publishes *Propositions of Philosophy*. It contains 190 essays on philosophy, logic, mechanics, astronomy, Sir Isaac Newton's theory of gravity, and the need for women's higher education. She is 20 years old.

1754   French mathematician Émilie du Châtelet publishes *Dissertation sur la nature et la propagation de feu* (Dissertation on the nature and propagation of fire).

1775–1783   The American Revolution. The Declaration of Independence is signed in July 1776.

1783   Caroline Herschel receives a telescope as a gift from her brother, astronomer William Herschel. During her career as an astronomer, Caroline will sight eight comets and fourteen nebulae.

1792   Plantation owner Catherine Littlefield Greene lends financial support to Eli Whitney so that he can develop a machine to separate cotton seeds from fiber and help speed up cotton production.

1811   British paleontologist Mary Anning discovers the complete fossilized remains of an ichthyosaur, a prehistoric marine reptile.

1816   Sophie Germain wins a gold medal from the French Academy of

Sciences for her essay explaining the results of an experiment in mathematical terms.

1833   Englishwoman Augusta Ada Lovelace begins helping mathematician Charles Babbage with his "Analytical Engine," an early computer.

1847   American astronomer Maria Mitchell discovers a new comet, which is subsequently named after her.

1848   The first women's rights convention is held in Seneca Falls, New York.

1861–1865   Civil War in America

1869   American astronomer Mary Watson Whitney is allowed to attend two classes at Harvard University, but she must wait outside the college gates for her professor, Benjamin Peirce, to escort her to the classroom, because Harvard isn't officially open to women.

1874   Russian mathematician Sofia Kovalevskaia becomes the first woman to receive a doctorate from a German university when she earns her Ph.D. from Göttingen University.

1881   Inventor Helen Augusta Blanchard founds the Blanchard Overseam Machine Company to produce her sewing machine inventions.

1883   The Brooklyn Bridge opens, joining New York City with Brooklyn (still an independent city). The project might never have been completed if Emily Roebling hadn't taken it over after her husband, engineer Washington Roebling, became too ill to supervise the work.

1884   Ellen Swallow Richards establishes the first sanitary chemistry laboratory and travels around the world to teach and help fellow engineers set up similar labs.

1892   Christine Ladd-Franklin introduces her theory of color vision. Her work is accepted during her lifetime, but she receives little recognition in the history of color theory.

1893   The World's Columbian Exhibition takes place in Chicago. Among the many items on display there are commercial dishwashers that were invented by Josephine Cochrane and architect Sophia Hayden's "Women's Building."

1894   Geologist Florence Bascom becomes the first woman elected as a fellow to the Geological Society of America.

Annie Jump Cannon

1896   Astronomer Annie Jump Cannon begins work at the Harvard College Observatory, where her colleagues include the esteemed astronomers Williamina Fleming, Antonia Maury, and Helen Leavitt.

1898   Chemist Marie Curie and her husband, Pierre Curie, discover the elements polonium and radium. Marie's work with radioactivity (a term she coined) will make her the first person ever to win two Nobel Prizes, one for physics in 1903 (with Pierre) and one for chemistry in 1911.

1903   The Wright Brothers, Orville and Wilbur, make the first successful flight in an airplane at Kitty Hawk, North Carolina.

1914–1918   World War I. Geologist Julia Gardner leaves her position with the United States Geological Survey and travels to France to join the war effort, serving first with the Red Cross and later with the American Friends Service Committee.

1915   Renowned German mathematician Emmy Noether is prohibited from lecturing in public by a law that excludes women from obtaining the necessary permit. She finally obtains the right in 1919.

1917   The Russian Revolution. The Russian Imperial family is executed, and the Russian Communist party is founded. Many women, including mathematician Nina Bari, benefit from new laws implemented after the revolution that provide for the integration of women students into the universities.

1920   The 19th Amendment to the United States Constitution grants women's suffrage. It goes into effect on August 26th. Among those responsible for the victory is civil engineer Nora Stanton Blatch Barney, who, like her mother (Harriot Stanton Blatch) and grandmother (Elizabeth Cady Stanton), is a suffragist.

1927   Mathematician Hilda Geiringer is appointed as an unsalaried lecturer at the University of Berlin. She is later forced to leave her position, along with other Jewish professors, after Hitler's rise to power.

1930   The New York City Women's Hospital is equipped with an

X-ray machine and radium for cancer patients.

1935
French physicists Irène and Frédéric Joliot-Curie earn the Nobel Prize in chemistry for their pioneering research in radiation. The couple have continued the work of Irène's parents, Marie and Pierre Curie.

1939–1945
World War II. The United States government suspects that the Germans are developing a new type of weapon—an atomic bomb. The U.S. officials assemble a group of scientists in Los Alamos, New Mexico, where they begin top-secret work on the Manhattan Project in an effort to build an atomic bomb first.

1939
French physicist Marguerite Perey discovers the element francium.

1941
Actress Hedy Lamarr collaborates with film composer George Antheil to create a remote-controlled radio system to produce transmissions that are indecipherable without the appropriate receiver. They patent the device and offer it to the U.S., but the War Department fails to use it.

1945
British scientist Kathleen Lonsdale is one of the first women to become a fellow of the Royal Society. She is recognized for her study of the structure of crystals.

1946
Mathematician Mina Rees is honored as the first female director of the American Association for the Advancement of Science.

1947
Chemist Dorothy Crowfoot Hodgkin is awarded a fellowship of the Royal Society for her work.

1949
After the explosion of an atomic bomb by the Soviet Union, the nuclear arms race between the United States and the Soviet Union begins.

1953
Computer scientist Evelyn Berezin designs the first office computer for the Underwood Corporation.

1958
Physicist Chien-Shiung Wu becomes the first woman ever to receive an honorary doctorate in science from Princeton University.

1963
German-born physicist Maria Goeppert Mayer, a researcher who helped determine the structure of the atomic nucleus, is one of the winners of the Nobel Prize in physics.

1964
British scientist Dorothy Crowfoot Hodgkin wins the Nobel Prize in chemistry for her work using X-ray techniques to determine the structure of penicillin and Vitamin B_{12}.

1964–1975
War in Vietnam. The United States enters the conflict as an ally of South Vietnam, battling communist forces in the North.

1966
Austrian physicists Lise Meitner, Otto Hahn, and Fritz Strassman are awarded the Enrico Fermi Prize for their collaborative work in nuclear fission.

Jocelyn Bell Burnell

1967
A pulsar (pulsating star) is discovered by radio astronomer Jocelyn Bell

Burnell, who is working under Antony Hewish.

1970
Inventor Beulah Henry receives her 49th patent at age 83.

1972
British astronomer Margaret Burbidge becomes the first female director of the Royal Greenwich Observatory. It is a prestigious appointment, but, unlike the male directors who preceded her, she is not given the honorary title of "astronomer royal."

1975
Mathematicians Evelyn Boyd Granville and Jason Frand publish their textbook, *Theory and Application of Mathematics for Teachers*.

1981
The IBM Corporation introduces the first personal computer, or PC—more than 100 years after Ada Lovelace and Charles Babbage had envisioned such a machine.

1983
Astronaut and physicist Sally Ride becomes the first American woman to travel into space. She spends six days in the shuttle *Challenger*, along with three male colleagues.

1984
Soviet cosmonaut Svetlana Savitskaya becomes the first woman ever to walk in space.

1985
Astronomer Carl Sagan publishes the science fiction novel *Contact*, based in part on the life and work of the astronomer Jill Cornell Tarter at the SETI (Search for Extraterrestrial Intelligence) Institute. In 1997 Sagan's book will be made into a movie starring Jodie Foster.

1992
Pioneering computer scientist Grace Murray Hopper dies. Her projects included developing operating programs for the first automatic, general-purpose digital calculator

Grace Murray Hopper

(the Harvard-IBM Mark I Automatic Sequence Controlled Calculator) in the 1940s.

1995
Mathematician Andrew Wise solves Pierre de Fermat's "Last Theorem," which states that there is no solution for the equation $x^n + y^n = z^n$. The 19th-century French mathematician Sophie Germain had found a limited proof for the theorem, but little else had been accomplished for more than a century, until now.

1996
After experimenting for 16 years, sculptor and inventor Patricia Billings creates GeoBond, a mixture of cement and gypsum. GeoBond, which is durable, fireproof, and nontoxic, could prove an alternative to asbestos.

1997
Space shuttle *Pathfinder* arrives on the planet Mars after a seven-month journey and releases the *Sojourner* probe to gather pictures and other data. *Sojourner*, which performs spectacularly, was designed by a NASA team led by aeronautical engineer Donna Shirley.

1999
Lene Vestergaard Hau and colleague Dr. Steve Harris at the Rowland Institute of Harvard University slow down the speed of light to 38 miles (61 km) per hour. In space, light travels at approximately 186,000 miles (299,330 km) per second.

GLOSSARY

Algebra: a branch of mathematics in which symbols, especially letters, are used to represent numbers and other values, so that operations involving several variables (rather than specific numbers) can be performed.

Alpha particle: a positively charged nuclear particle that is made up of two protons and two neutrons and is spontaneously released during radioactive decay. An alpha ray is a stream of alpha particles.

Applied mathematics: the use of mathematical principles to solve practical problems in fields such as physics, engineering, and biology. In contrast, "pure" or abstract mathematics focuses on the formulation and proof of theoretical problems.

Atom: the smallest possible unit of an element that displays the chemical properties of that element. It contains a nucleus, made up of protons and neutrons, which is surrounded by a cloud of electrons.

Calculus: a method of calculating, especially as applied to continuous functions. In differential calculus, the focus is on analyzing the rate of change of one variable with respect to another, for example, calculating velocity (an object's speed with respect to time traveled). In integral calculus, the basic focus is on measurement, such as determining the length of a curve or volume of a sphere.

Chemistry: the study of substances—their composition, fundamental structure, and the ways they react in combination with other substances.

Compound: in chemistry, a pure substance resulting from the union of two or more elements. For example, water (H_2O) is a compound made up of molecules that each contain two hydrogen atoms bound to one oxygen atom.

Constellation: in astronomy, a group of stars that has been given a name. Early star-watchers often perceived the patterns formed by stars as pictures. For that reason many constellations are named after an object, mythological figure, or animal.

Corona: a circle of light that can sometimes be seen around a luminous celestial body such as the moon, sun, or stars. Also, the outermost atmosphere of the sun, which is made up of hot, electrically charged gas and is best viewed during a solar eclipse.

Electron: a negatively charged subatomic particle with almost negligible mass; an electron weighs 1,800 times less than an atom of hydrogen, the lightest element. Electrons are normally found orbiting the nucleus of an atom, although they can exist separately in a matter known as plasma.

Element: a substance that cannot be reduced to a simpler form through normal chemical processes. All matter is composed of elements, either singly or in combination (as compounds).

Fossil: a trace or impression of a prehistoric life-form that has been preserved, often through petrification (conversion into mineral matter), in the crust of the Earth. Bony animals, shellfish, plants, and insects are among the most common fossils.

Geology: the study of the physical history, composition, and structure of Earth through the examination of rocks and other materials that make up the planet. Also the similar study of celestial bodies such as the moon and stars.

Isotope: one of two or more forms of atoms in a chemical element that have the same number of protons but differing numbers of neutrons. Different isotopes display almost identical chemical properties but do not have the same atomic masses.

Light-year: an astronomical unit of length that is equal to the distance traveled by light moving through space for the period of one year: approximately 5.878 trillion miles (9.46 trillion km).

Microprocessor: a tiny electronic device that contains the programming and circuitry necessary to perform as the central processing unit—interpreting and executing commands—for a digital computer.

Molecule: the smallest unit into which a substance can be broken down and still retain its identifying chemical properties. A molecule of an element would contain only one atom; that of a compound would contain two or more atoms bound together.

Neutron: a subatomic particle that has no electronic charge and weighs slightly more than a proton. It is present in all known atomic nuclei except the hydrogen nucleus.

Nucleus: in physics, the central region of an atom, made up of protons and neutrons and surrounded by electrons.

Ore: a mineral or rock from which a valuable substance—usually metal—can be extracted.

Paleontology: the study of ancient life-forms through the examination of fossil remains.

Petrology: the study of the origin, chemical composition, and classification of rocks.

Physics: the study of the properties and interactions of matter and energy and their effects in the observable world.

Prism: a transparent object, usually glass, that is cut into precise angles and used to reflect and analyze light. The most common prism, a triangular shape, separates white light into its spectrum, an array of all the colors that make up the light beam.

Proton: a subatomic particle that has a positive electrical charge and is found in the nucleus of all atoms.

Quantum mechanics: a modern branch of physics that seeks to account for the behavior of atoms and subatomic particles. It is based upon the idea that energy and momentum can be "quantized," or

assigned a particular set of measurable units that help to explain occurrences at this extremely small scale, where the physical laws of the larger world do not apply.

Radioactivity: the property of some elements (such as uranium), whereby they spontaneously emit energy in the form of subatomic rays, such as alpha rays, as their atomic nuclei disintegrate.

Specific gravity: also known as relative density. The ratio of the density of one substance as compared to that of a substance that has been chosen as a standard. Water at a temperature of 4° Celsius (39° F) provides the usual standard for determining the specific gravity of liquids and solids. So, for example, a substance with a specific gravity of 3 would weigh three times as much as the same volume of water.

Spectroscope: a device used to reveal light spectra for observation and study. Spectroscopy is the use of such a device.

Spectrum (plural, spectra): in optics (the study of visible and invisible light), the arrangement of light waves in order of their length. The spectrum is revealed as bands of color when a beam of light is passed through a prism (there are also wavelengths that aren't visible to the naked eye). Sunlight (or white light) contains the full visible spectrum: red (with the longest wavelength), orange, yellow, green, blue, indigo, and violet (with the shortest wavelength).

Stratigraphy: a branch of geology that deals with the interpretation and classification of stratified (many-layered) rock. By examining different strata, or layers, stratigraphers can learn how and when the rock was formed and whether valuable substances such as oil are likely to be found nearby.

Thermodynamics: a branch of physics that deals with heat and other types of energy and their relationship to mechanical work, or motion.

X ray: electromagnetic radiation of short wavelengths. The ability of X rays to pass through many solid substances allows for hidden objects, such as bones and organs within the body, to be photographed.

INDEX

Numbers in boldface type indicate main entries.

CREDITS

Quotes

16 Boole, Mary Everest. *Lectures on the Logic of Arithmetic*. Oxford: Clarendon Press, 1903. **27** GABe, Frances. "The GABe Self-Cleaning House" from Zimmerman, Jan (ed.) *The Technological Woman: Interfacing with Tomorrow*. New York: Praeger Special Studies, 1983. Used by permission. **30** Grandin, Temple. *Thinking in Pictures: And Other Reports from My Life with Autism*. © 1995 by Temple Grandin. Used by permission of Doubleday, a division of Random House, Inc. **43** Lavoisier, Marie. From *Travels in France and Italy During the Years 1787, 1788, and 1789*, by Arthur Young. London: J. M. Dent, 1927. **54** Payne-Gaposchkin, Cecilia. *Cecilia Payne-Gaposchkin: An Autobiography and Other Recollections*. Cambridge: Cambridge University Press, 1984. Used by permission of Cambridge University Press. **55** Péter, Rósza. *Playing with Infinity: Mathematics for Everyman*. New York: Simon and Schuster, 1962.

Photographs

Abbreviations

AIP	American Institute of Physics
COR	Corbis
HCO	Harvard College Observatory
HG	Hulton Getty
LOC	Library of Congress

8 (and title page) Agnesi, Maria, LOC. **10** Ayrton, Hertha, LOC. **11** Bascom, Florence, Bryn Mawr Archives. **12** Bassi, Laura, LOC. **14** Bishop, Hazel, LOC. **15** Blanchard, Helen, LOC; Blodgett, Katherine, LOC. **17** Burbidge, Margaret, HG. **18** Carr, Emma, LOC. **19** Châtelet, Émilie, from Houssaye, M. Arsène. *Les Femmes du Temps Passé*. Paris: Morizot, Libraire-Éditeur, no date. **21 (and cover)** Curie, Marie, HG; Dennis, Olive, LOC. **22** Dresselhaus, Mildred, Donna Coveney/MIT. **23** Einstein, Mileva, HG. **24 (and cover)** Falconer, Etta, courtesy of Etta Falconer. **25** Fleming, Williamina, HCO. **26** Fu, Beatrice, courtesy of Tensilica, Inc. **29** Geller, Margaret, COR/Roger Ressmeyer; **(and 7)** Gilbreth, Lillian, LOC. **31 (and 7)** Granville, Evelyn, courtesy of Evelyn Granville; Gray, Mary, courtesy of Mary Gray. **32** Griffin, Marion, © Collection of The New-York Historical Society. **33 (and cover)** Hau, Lene, courtesy of MaryAnn Nilsson/Rowland Institute for Science. **35** Herschel, Caroline, LOC; Hicks, Beatrice, LOC. **36** Hodgkin, Dorothy, LOC. **38** Jackson, Shirley, Schomburg Center; Joliot-Curie, Irène, HG. **40** Kovalevskaia, Sonya, HG. **42** Ladd-Franklin, Christine, from Cirker, Hayward & Blanche (eds). *Dictionary of American Portraits*. New York: Dover Publications, Inc., 1967; Lamarr, Hedy, LOC. **44** Leavitt, Henrietta, HCO. **45** Libby, Leona, Brookhaven National Laboratory, Photography Division, courtesy AIP. **46** Lonsdale, Kathleen, HG. **47** Lucid, Shannon, LOC. **49** Maury, Antonia, HCO. **50** Meitner, Lise, HG; Mitchell, Maria, LOC. **51** Morgan, Julia, Special Collections, California Polytechnic State University. **53 (and title page)** Ocampo, Adriana, NASA; Ochoa, Ellen, NASA. **55** Perey, Marguerite, AIP. **56** Quimby, Edith, AIP. **57** Rees, Mina, LOC; Reiche, Maria, COR/Bettmann. **59 (and title page)** Richards, Ellen, LOC; Riddle, Theodate, courtesy of the Hillstead Museum. **60 (and cover)** Ride, Sally, NASA. **61 (and 6)** Roebling, Emily, LOC. **62** Savitskaya, Svetlana, COR/Bettmann. **63 (and 6)** Shirley, Donna, NASA. **64** Somerville, Mary, HG. **66** Telkes, Maria, LOC; Tharp, Marie, LOC. **67** Van Straten, Florence, LOC; Wheeler, Anna, Bryn Mawr Archives. **69** Wright, Jessie, LOC; **(and title page)** Wu, Chien-Shiung, LOC. **70** Young, Grace, courtesy of Sylvia Wiegand. **71** Hypatia, LOC. **73** Cannon, Annie, HCO. **74** Bell Burnell, Jocelyn, The Open University, courtesy AIP. **75** Hopper, Grace Murray, LOC.